The Lay of the Cid:
Translated into English Verse

by

R. Selden Rose and Leonard Bacon

The Echo Library 2007

Published by

The Echo Library

Echo Library
131 High St.
Teddington
Middlesex TW11 8HH

www.echo-library.com

Please report serious faults in the text to complaints@echo-library.com

ISBN 978-1-40684-620-1

THE CID

Lashed in the saddle, the Cid thundered out
To his last onset. With a strange disdain
The dead man looked on victory. In vain
Emir and Dervish strive against the rout.
In vain Morocco and Biserta shout,
For still before the dead man fall the slain.
Death rides for Captain of the Men of Spain,
And their dead truth shall slay the living doubt.

The soul of the great epic, like the chief,
Conquers in aftertime on fields unknown.
Men hear today the horn of Roland blown
To match the thunder of the guns of France,
And nations with a heritage of grief
Follow their dead victorious in Romance.

4

INTRODUCTION

The importance of the Cid as Spain's bulwark against the Moors of the eleventh century is exceeded by his importance to his modern countrymen as the epitome of the noble and vigorous qualities that made Spain great. Menéndez y Pelayo has called him the symbol of Spanish nationality in virtue of the fact that in him there were united sobriety of intention and expression, simplicity at once noble and familiar, ingenuous and easy courtesy, imagination rather solid than brilliant, piety that was more active than contemplative, genuine and soberly restrained affections, deep conjugal devotion, a clear sense of justice, loyalty to his sovereign tempered by the courage to protest against injustice to himself, a strange and appealing confusion of the spirit of chivalry and plebeian rudeness, innate probity rich in vigorous and stern sincerity, and finally a vaguely sensible delicacy of affection that is the inheritance of strong men and clean blood. [1]

This is the epic Cid who in the last quarter of the eleventh century was banished by Alphonso VI of Castile, fought his way to the Mediterranean, stormed Valencia, married his two daughters to the Heirs of Carrión and defended his fair name in parliament and in battle.

The poet either from ignorance or choice has disregarded the historical significance of the campaigns of the Cid. He fails to mention his defeat of the threatening horde of Almoravides at the very moment when their victory over Alphonso's Castilians at Zalaca had opened to them Spain's richest provinces, and turns the crowning achievement of the great warrior's life into the preliminary to a domestic event which he considered of greater importance. We are grateful to him for his lack of accuracy, for it illustrates how men thought about their heroes in that time. The twelfth century Castilians would have admitted that in battle the Cid was of less avail than their patron James, the son of Zebedee, but they would have added that after all the saint was a Galilean and not a Spaniard.

In order then to make the Cid not merely heroic but a national hero he must become the possessor of attributes of greatness beyond mere courage. The poet therefore, probably assuming that his hearers were well aware of the Cid's prowess in arms, devoted himself to a theme of more intimate appeal. The Cid, an exile from Castile and flouted by his enemies at home, must vindicate himself. The discomfiture of the Moor is not an end in itself but the means of vindication and, be it said, of support. When he is restored to favor, the marriage of his daughters to the Heirs of Carrión under Alphonso's auspices is the royal acknowledgment. The treachery of the heirs is the pretext for the Parliament of Toledo where the Cid shall appear in all the glory of triumphant vindication. The interest in the hecatombs of Moors and even in the fall of Valencia is a secondary one. What really matters is that the Cid's fair name be

---

[1] Cf. Menéndez y Pelayo, Tratado de los romances viejos, I, 315.

cleared of all stain of disloyalty and the doña Elvira and doña Sol wed worthy husbands.

This unity of plan is consistently preserved by a rearrangement of the true chronology of events and by the introduction of purely traditional episodes. The shifting of historical values may be due to the fact that when the poem was composed, about 1150, the power of the Moor had really been broken by the conquests of Ferdinand I, Alphonso VI, Alphonso VII and Alphonso VIII of Castile and alphonso I, the Battler, of Aragon. The menace was no longer felt with the keenness of an hundred years before. until the end of the tenth century the Moors had dominated the Peninsula. The growth of the Christian states from the heroic nucleus in northern Asturias was confined to the territory bordering the Bay of Biscay, Asturias, Santander, part of the province of Burgos, León, and Galicia. In the East other centers of resistance had sprung up in Navarre, Aragon and the County of Barcelona. At the beginning of the eleventh century the tide turned. The progress of the reconquest was due as much to the disruption of Moorish unity as to the greater aggressiveness and closer coöperation of the Christian kingdoms. The end of the Caliphate of Cordova was the signal for the rise of a great number of mutually independent Moorish states. Sixty years later there were no less than twenty- three of them. By the middle of the following century the enthusiasm that had followed the first successful blows struck against the Moor had waned, and with it the vividness of their historical significance and order.

Let us look at the Cid for a moment as he was seen by a Latin chronicler who confesses that the purpose of his modest narrative was merely to preserve the memory of the Cid of history.

When Ferdinand I of Castile died under the walls of Valencia in 1065 he divided his kingdom among his five children. To Sancho he left Castile, to Alphonso León, to García Galicia, to doña Urraca the city and lands of Zamora, and to doña Elvira Toro. Sancho, like his father, soon set about uniting the scattered inheritance. Ruy Diaz, a native of Bivar near Burgos, was his standard bearer against Alphonso at the battle of Volpéjar, aided him in the Galician campaign and was active at the siege of Zamora, where Sancho was treacherously slain. Alphonso, the despoiled lord of León, succeeded to the throne of Castile. Ruy Diaz, now called the Campeador (Champion) in honor of his victory over a knight of Navarre, was sent with a force of men to collect the annual taxes from the tributary Moorish kings of Andalusia. Mudafar of Granada, eager to throw off the yoke of Castile, marched against the Campeador and the loyal Motamid of Seville, and was routed at the battle of Cabra. García Ordoñez who was fighting in the ranks of Mudafar was taken prisoner. It was here probably that the Cid acquired that tuft of García's beard which he later produced with such convincing effect at Toledo. The Cid returned to Castile laden with booty and honors. The jealousy aroused by this exploit and by an equally successful raid against the region about Toledo caused the banishment of the Cid. From this time until his death he was ceaselessly occupied in warfare against the Moors.

The way to Valencia was beset with more and greater difficulties than those described in the poem. The events of the first years of exile are closely associated with the moorish state of Zaragoza. At the death of its sovereign Almoktadir bitter strife arose between his two sons, Almutamin in Zaragoza and Alfagib in Denia. The Cid and his followers cast their lot with the former, while Alfagib sought in vain to maintain the balance by allying himself with Sancho of Aragon and Berenguer of Barcelona. After a decisive victory in which Berenguer was taken prisoner Almutamin returned to Zaragoza with his champion, "honoring him above his own son, his realm and all his possessions, so that he seemed almost the lord of the kingdom." There the Cid continued to increase in wealth and fame at the expense of Sancho of Aragon and Alfagib until the death of Almutamin.

For a short time the Cid was restored to the good graces of Alphonso, but a misunderstanding during some joint military expedition brought a second decree of banishment. The Cid's possessions were confiscated and his wife and children cast into prison.

The Cid then went to the support of Alkaadir, king of Valencia. He defeated the threatening Almoravides flushed with their victory over the Castilians at Zalaca. Again he chastised Berenguer of Barcelona. he hastened to answer a second summons from Alphonso, this time to bear aid in operations in the region about Granada. Suspecting that Alphonso intended treachery, he with drew from the camp toward Valencia. With Zaragoza as his base he laid waste the lands of Sancho and avenged himself upon Alphonso by ravaging Calahorra and Nájera.

Finally in 1092 the overthrow of Alkaadir prompted him to interfere definitely in the affairs of Valencia. He besieged the city closely and captured it in 1094. There he ruled, independent, until his death in 1099.

Even the Moorish chroniclers of the twelfth century pay their tribute to the memory of the Cid by the virulence of their hatred. Aben Bassam wrote: "The might of this tyrant was ever growing until its weight was felt upon the highest peaks and in the deepest valleys, and filled with terror both noble and commoner. I have heard men say that when his eagerness was greatest and his ambition highest he uttered these words, 'If one Rodrigo brought ruin upon this Peninsula, another Rodrigo shall reconquer it!' A saying that filled the hearts of the believers with fear and caused them to think that what they anxiously dreaded would speedily come to pass. This man, who was the lash and scourge of his time, was, because of his love of glory, his steadfastness of character and his heroic valor, one of the miracles of the Lord. Victory ever followed Rodrigo's banner—may Allay curse him—he triumphed over the princes of the unbelievers…and with a handful of men confounded and dispersed their numerous armies.' [2] One can hardly look for strict neutrality in the verdicts of Moorish historians, but between the one extreme of fanaticism that led Aben

---

[2] Aben Bassam, Tesoro (1109), cf. Dozy, Recherches sur l'histoire politique et littéraire d'Espagne pendant le Moyen Age. Leyden, 1849.

Bassam elsewhere to call the Cid a robber and a Galician dog and the other that four centuries later urged his canonization, the true believer can readily discern the figure of a warrior who was neither saint nor bandit.

The deeds of such a man naturally appealed to popular imagination, and it is not wonderful that there were substantial accretions that less than a hundred years later found their way into the Epic. Within an astonishingly short time the purely traditional elements of the marriage of the Cid's daughters and the Parliament at Toledo became its central theme. It is probable that such a vital change was not entirely due to conscious art in a poet whose distinguishing characteristic is his very unconsciousness. From his minute familiarity with the topography of the country about Medina and Gormaz, his affection for St. Stephen's, his utter lack of accuracy in his description of the siege of Valencia and from the disproportionate prominence given to such really insignificant episodes as the sieges of Castejón and Alcocer, Pidal has inferred that the unknown poet was himself a native of this region and that his story of the life of the Cid is the product of local tradition.[3] Moreover there is abundant evidence to prove that before the composition of the poem as it has come down to us, the compelling figure of the Cid had inspired other chants of an heroic if not epic nature.

From this vigorous plant patriotic fervor and sympathetic imagination caused to spring a perennial growth of popular legends. The "General Chronicle of Alphonso the Wise," begun in 1270, reflects the national affection for the very chattels of the Cid. it relates that Babiéca passed the evening of his life in ease and luxury and that his seed flourished in the land.

After this constantly increasing biographical material had been developed and expanded through at least six chronicles and later epic treatment it was taken up by the ballads with a wealth of new episodes. Of these one of the most interesting is the Cid's duel with the conde Lozano and his marriage to Ximena. The hounds of Diego Lainez, the Cid's father, have seized a hare belonging to the conde Lozano, who considers that he has been grievously insulted thereby. Accordingly he retaliates with slurs that can removed only ont he field of honor. Diego Lainez, too old to fight, in order to discover which one of his three sons is worthy of clearing the honor of the family, bites the finger of each one successively. The two eldest utter only cries of pain, but Rodrigo with great spirit threatens his father. He is chosen to fight the conde Lozano and slays him. Ximena demands justice for her father's death, and protection. Thereupon by order of King Ferdinand the Cid and Ximena are married. Later we have Ximena's complaints that her husband's activity in the field against the Moors have tried her spirit sorely. There are many ballads that treat of the arming and consecration of the Cid in newly conquered Coimbra, of his victory over five Moorish kings who gave him the name Cid (Master), and became his tributaries, of the testament of Ferdinand in virtue of which the Cid is made the adviser of Sancho and Urraca. The siege of Zamora and the death of Sancho are fertile

---

[3] Cid, 1, 72-73.

topics. At the accession of Alphonso the Cid forces him to swear a solemn oath that he was not party to the murder of his brother Sancho. Finally when the Cid is independent master of Valencia, the Sultan of Persia, hearing of his exploits, sends him rich presents and a magic balsam. This the Cid drinks when he is at the point of death. It preserves his dead body with such perfect semblance of life that, mounted on Babiéca, he turns the victory of the Moor Bucar into utter rout.

Not the least curious is the legend of the Jew who having feared the living Cid, desired to pluck his sacred beard as he lay in state in St. Peter's at Cardena. "This is the body of the Cid," said he, "so praised of all, and men say that while he lived none plucked his beard. I would fain seize it and take it in my hand, for since he lies here dead he shall not prevent this." The Jew stretched forth his hand, but ere he touched that beard the Cid laid his hand upon his sword Tizóna and drew it forth from its scabbard a handsbreadth. When the Jew beheld this he was struck with mighty fear, and backward he fell in a swoon for terror. Now this Jew was converted and ended his days in St. Peter's, a man of God.

The uninitiated reader will doubtless miss in the Epic more than one of his most fondly cherished episodes. If he prefer the Cid of romance and fable, let him turn to the ballads and the Chronicle of the Cid. If he would cling to the punctilious, gallant hidalgo of the early seventeenth century, let him turn to the Cid of Guillem de Castro, or to Corneille's paragon. Don Quixote wisely said: "That there was a Cid there is no doubt, or Bernardo del Carpio either; but that they did the deeds men say they did, there is a doubt a-plenty." In the heroic heart of the Epic Cid one finds the simple nobility that later centuries have obscured with adornment.

CANTAR I

THE BANISHMENT OF THE CID

I.

He turned and looked upon them, and he wept very sore
As he saw the yawning gateway and the hasps wrenched off the door,
And the pegs whereon no mantle nor coat of vair there hung.
There perched no moulting goshawk, and there no falcon swung.
My lord the Cid sighed deeply such grief was in his heart
And he spake well and wisely:
"Oh Thou, in Heaven that art
Our Father and our Master, now I give thanks to Thee.
Of their wickedness my foemen have done this thing to me."

II.

Then they shook out the bridle rein further to ride afar.
They had the crow on their right hand as they issued from Bivár;
And as they entered Burgos upon their left it sped.
And the Cid shrugged his shoulders, and the Cid shook his head:
"Good tidings, Alvar Fañez. We are banished from our weal,
But on a day with honor shall we come unto Castile."

III.

Roy Diaz entered Burgos with sixty pennons strong,
And forth to look upon him did the men and women throng.
And with their wives the townsmen at the windows stood hard by,
And they wept in lamentation, their grief was risen so high.
As with one mouth, together they spake with one accord:
"God, what a noble vassal, an he had a worthy lord.

IV.

Fain had they made him welcome, but none dared do the thing
For fear of Don Alfonso, and the fury of the King.
His mandate unto Burgos came ere the evening fell.
With utmost care they brought it, and it was sealed well
'That no man to Roy Diaz give shelter now, take heed
And if one give him shelter, let him know in very deed
He shall lose his whole possession, nay! the eyes within his head
Nor shall his soul and body be found in better stead.'

Great sorrow had the Christians, and from his face they hid.
Was none dared aught to utter unto my lord the Cid.

Then the Campeador departed unto his lodging straight.
But when he was come thither, they had locked and barred the gate.
In their fear of King Alfonso had they done even so.
An the Cid forced not his entrance, neither for weal nor woe
Durst they open it unto him. Loudly his men did call.
Nothing thereto in answer said the folk within the hall.
My lord the Cid spurred onward, to the doorway did he go.
He drew his foot from the stirrup, he smote the door one blow.
Yet the door would not open, for they had barred it fast.
But a maiden of nine summers came unto him at last:

"Campeador, in happy hour thou girdedst on the sword.
'This the King's will. Yestereven came the mandate of our lord.
With utmost care they brought it, and it was sealed with care:
None to ope to you or greet you for any cause shall dare.
And if we do, we forfeit houses and lands instead.
Nay we shall lose, moreover, the eyes within the head
And, Cid, with our misfortune, naught whatever dost thou gain.
But may God with all his power support thee in thy pain."

So spake the child and turned away. Unto her home went she.
That he lacked the King's favor now well the Cid might see.
He left the door; forth onward he spurred through Burgos town.
When he had reached Saint Mary's, then he got swiftly down
He fell upon his knee and prayed with a true heart indeed:
and when the prayer was over, he mounted on the steed.
North from the gate and over the Arlanzon he went.
Here in the sand by Burgos, the Cid let pitch his tent.
Roy Diaz, who in happy hour had girded on the brand,
Since none at home would greet him, encamped there on the sand.
With a good squadron, camping as if within the wood.
They will not let him in Burgos buy any kind of food.
Provender for a single day they dared not to him sell.

V.

Good Martin Antolínez in Burgos that did dwell
To the Cid and to his henchmen much wine and bread gave o'er,
That he bought not, but brought with him—of everything good store.

Content was the great Campeador, and his men were of good cheer.
Spake Martin Antolínez. His counsel you shall hear.

"In happy hour, Cid Campeador, most surely wast thou born.
Tonight here let us tarry, but let us flee at morn,
For someone will denounce me, that thy service I have done.
In the danger of Alfonso I certainly shall run.
Late or soon, if I 'scape with thee the King must seek me forth
For friendship's sake; if not, my wealth, a fig it is not worth.

VI.

Then said the Cid, who in good hour had girded on the steel:
"Oh Martin Antolínez, thou art a good lance and leal.
And if I live, hereafter I shall pay thee double rent,
But gone is all my silver, and all my gold is spent.
And well enough thou seest that I bring naught with me
And many things are needful for my good company.
Since by favor I win nothing by might then must I gain.
I desire by thy counsel to get ready coffers twain.
With the sand let us fill them, to lift a burden sore,
And cover them with stamped leather with nails well studded o'er.

VII.

Ruddy shall be the leather, well gilded every nail.
In my behalf do thou hasten to Vidas and Raquél.
Since in Burgos they forbade me aught to purchase, and the King
Withdraws his favor, unto them my goods I cannot bring.
They are heavy, and I must pawn them for whatso'er is right.
That Christians may not see it, let them come for them by night.
May the Creator judge it and of all the Saints the choir.
I can no more, and I do it against my own desire."

VIII.

Martin stayed not. Through Burgos he hastened forth, and came
To the Castle. Vidas and Raquél, he demanded them by name.

IX.

Raquél and Vidas sate to count their goods and profits through,
When up came Antolínez, the prudent man and true.

"How now Raquél and Vidas, am I dear unto your heart,
I would speak close." They tarried not. All three they went apart.
"Give me, Raquél and Vidas, your hands for promise sure
That you will not betray me to Christian or to Moor.

I shall make you rich forever. You shall ne'er be needy more.
When to gather in the taxes went forth the Campeador,
Many rich goods he garnered, but he only kept the best.
Therefore this accusation against him was addressed.
And now two mighty coffers full of pure gold hath he.
Why he lost the King's favor a man may lightly see.
He has left his halls and houses, his meadow and his field,
And the chests he cannot bring you lest he should stand revealed.
The Campeador those coffers will deliver to your trust.
And do you lend unto him whatsoever may be just.
Do you take the chests and keep them, but swear a great oath here
That you will not look within them for the space of all this year."

The two took counsel:
"Something to our profit must inure
In all barter. He gained something in the country of the Moor
When he marched there, for many goods he brought with him away.
But he sleeps not unsuspected, who brings coined gold to pay.
Let the two of us together take now the coffers twain.
In some place let us put them where unseen they shall remain.

"What the lord Cid demandeth, we prithee let us hear,
And what will be our usury for the space of all this year?"

Said Martin Antolínez like a prudent man and true:
"Whatever you deem right and just the Cid desires of you.
He will ask little since his goods are left in a safe place.
But needy men on all sides beseech the Cid for grace.
For six hundred marks of money, the Cid is sore bested."

"We shall give them to him gladly," Raquél and Vidas said.

"'Tis night. The Cid is sorely pressed. So give the marks to us.
Answered Raquél and Vidas: "Men do not traffic thus.
But first they take their surety and thereafter give the fee."
Said Martin Antolínez:
"So be it as for me.
Come ye to the great Campeador for 'tis but just and fair
That we should help you with the chests, and put them in your care,
So that neither Moor nor Christian thereof shall hear the tale."

"Therewith are we right well content," said Vidas and Raquél,
"You shall have marks six hundred when we bring the chests again."

And Martin Antolínez rode forth swiftly with the twain.

And they were glad exceeding. O'er the bridge he did not go,
But through the stream, that never a Burgalese should know
Through him thereof. And now behold the Campeador his tent.
When they therein had entered to kiss his hands they bent.
My lord the Cid smiled on them and unto them said he:

"Ha, don Raquél and Vidas, you have forgotten me!
And now must I get hence away who am banished in disgrace,
For the king from me in anger hath turned away his face.
I deem that from my chattels you shall gain somewhat of worth.
And you shall lack for nothing while you dwell upon the earth.'

A-kissing of his hands forthwith Raquél and Vidas fell.
Good Martin Antolínez had made the bargain well,
That to him on the coffers marks six hundred they should lend.
And keep them safe, moreover, till the year had made an end.
For so their word was given and sworn to him again,
If they looked ere that within them, forsworn should be the twain,
The Cid would never give them one groat of usury.

Said Martin, "Let the chests be ta'en as swiftly as may be,
Take them, Raquél and Vidas, and keep them in your care.
And we shall even go with you that the money we may bear,
For ere the first cock croweth must my lord the Cid depart."

At the loading of the coffers you had seen great joy of heart.
For they could not heave the great chests up though they were stark and
    hale.
Dear was the minted metal to Vidas and Raquél;
And they would be rich forever till their two lives it were o'er

X.

The hand of my good lord the Cid, Raquél had kissed once more:
"Ha! Campeador, in happy hour thou girdedst on the brand.
Forth from Castile thou goest to the men of a strange land.
Such is become thy fortune and great thy gain shall be
Ah Cid, I kiss thine hands again—but make a gift to me
Bring me a Moorish mantle splendidly wrought and red."
"So be it. It is granted," the Cid in answer said,
"If from abroad I bring it, well doth the matter stand;
If not, take it from the coffers I leave here in your hand."

And then Raquél and Vidas bore the two chests away.
With Martin Antolínez into Burgos entered they.

And with fitting care, and caution unto their dwelling sped.
And in the midmost of the hall a plaited quilt they spread.
And a milk-white cloth of linen thereon did they unfold.
Three hundred marks of silver before them Martin told.
And forthwith Martin took them, no whit the coins he weighed.
Then other marks three hundred in gold to him they paid.
Martin had five esquires. He loaded all and one.
You shall hear what said don Martin when all this gear was done:

"Ha! don Raquél and Vidas, ye have the coffers two.
Well I deserve a guerdon, who obtained this prize for you."

XI.

Together Vidas and Raquél stepped forth apart thereon:
"Let us give him a fair present for our profit he has won.
Good Martin Antolínez in Burgos that dost dwell,
We would give thee a fair present for thou deserves well.
Therewith get breeches and a cloak and mantle rich and fine.
Thou hast earned it. For a present these thirty marks are thine.
For it is but just and honest, and, moreover, thou wilt stand
Our warrant in this bargain whereto we set our hand."

Don Martin thanked them duly and took the marks again.
He yearned to leave the dwelling and well he wished the twain.
He is gone out from Burgos. O'er the Arlanzon he went.
And him who in good hour was born he found within his tent.

The Cid arose and welcomed him, with arms held wide apart:
"Thou art come, Antolínez, good vassal that thou art!
May you live until the season when you reap some gain of me."

"Here have I come, my Campeador, with as good heed as might be.
Thou hast won marks six hundred, and thirty more have I.
Ho! order that they strike the tents and let us swiftly fly.
In San Pedro de Cardeñas let us hear the cock ere day.
We shall see your prudent lady, but short shall be our stay.
And it is needful for us from the kingdom forth to wend,
For the season of our suffrance drawns onward to its end."

XII.

They spake these words and straightaway the tent upgathered then,
My lord the Cid rode swiftly with all his host of men.
And forth unto Saint Mary's the horse's head turned he,
And with his right hand crossed himself: "God, I give thanks to thee
Heaven and Earth that rulest. And thy favor be my weal
Holy Saint Mary, for forthright must I now quit Castile.
For I look on the King with anger, and I know not if once more
I shall dwell there in my life-days. But may thy grace watch o'er
My parting, Blessed Virgin, and guard me night and day.
If thou do so and good fortune come once more in my way,
I will offer rich oblations at thine altar, and I swear
Most solemnly that I will chant a thousand masses there."

XIII.

And the lord Cid departed fondly as a good man may.
Forthwith they loosed the horses, and out they spurred away.
Said good Martin Antolínez in Burgos that did dwell:
"I would see my lady gladly and advise my people well
What they shall do hereafter. It matters not to me
Though the King take all. Ere sunrise I shall come unto thee."

XIV.

Martin went back to Burgos but my lord the Cid spurred on
To San Pedro of Cardeñas as hard as horse could run,
With all his men about him who served him as is due.
And it was nigh to morning, and the cocks full oft they crew,
When at last my lord the Campeador unto San Pedro came.
God's Christian was the Abbot. Don Sancho was his name;
And he was saying matins at the breaking of the day.
With her five good dames in waiting Xiména there did pray.
They prayed unto Saint Peter and God they did implore:
"O thou who guidest all mankind, succor the Campeador."

XV.

One knocked at the doorway, and they heard the tidings then.
God wot the Abbot Sancho was the happiest of men.
With the lights and with the candles to the court they ran forth right,
And him who in good hour was born they welcomed in delight.

"My lord Cid," quoth the Abbot, "Now God be praised of grace!

Do thou accept my welcome, since I see thee in this place."
And the Cid who in good hour was born, hereunto answered he:

"My thanks to thee, don Sancho, I am content with thee.
For myself and for my vassals provision will I make.
Since I depart to exile, these fifty marks now take.
If I may live my life-span, they shall be doubled you.
To the Abbey not a groatsworth of damage will I do.
For my lady do I give you an hundred marks again,
Herself, her dames and daughters for this year do you maintain.
I leave two daughters with you, but little girls they be.
In thine arms keep them kindly. I commend them here to thee.
Don Sancho do thou guard them, and of my wife take care.
If thou wantest yet and lackest for anything whate'er,
Look well to their provision, thee I conjure once more,
And for one mark that thou spendest the Abbey shall have four."
And with glad heart the Abbot his full assent made plain.
And lo! the Dame Xiména came with her daughters twain.
Each had her dame-in-waiting who the little maiden bore.
And Dame Xiména bent the knee before the Campeador.
And fain she was to kiss his hand, and, oh, she wept forlorn!

"A boon! A boon! my Campeador. In a good hour wert thou born.
And because of wicked slanderers art thou banished from the land.

XVI.

"Oh Campeador fair-bearded, a favor at thy hand!
Behold I kneel before thee, and thy daughters are here with me,
That have seen of days not many, for children yet they be,
And these who are my ladies to serve my need that know.
Now well do I behold it, thou art about to go.
Now from thee our lives a season must sunder and remove,
But unto us give succor for sweet Saint Mary's love."

The Cid, the nobly bearded, reached down unto the twain,
And in his arms his daughters has lifted up again,
And to his heart he pressed them, so great his love was grown,
And his tears fell fast and bitter, and sorely did he moan:
"Xiména as mine own spirit I loved thee, gentle wife;
But o'er well dost thou behold it, we must sunder in our life.
I must flee and thou behind me here in the land must stay.
Please God and sweet Saint Mary that yet upon a day
I shall give my girls in marriage with mine own hand rich and well,
And thereafter in good fortune be suffered yet to dwell,

May they grant me, wife, much honored, to serve thee then once more."

XVII.

A mighty feast they had prepared for the Great Campeador
The bells within San Pedro they clamor and they peal.
That my lord the Cid is banished men cry throughout Castile.
And some have left their houses, from their lands some fled away.
Of knights an hundred and fifteen were seen upon that day,
By the bridge across the Arlanzon together they came o'er.
One and all were they calling on the Cid Campeador.
And Martin Antolínez has joined him with their power.
They sought him in San Pedro, who was born in a good hour.

XVIII.

When that his host was growing, heard the great Cid of Bivár,
Swift he rode forth to meet them, for his fame would spread afar.
When they were come before him, he smiled on them again.
And one and all drew near him and to kiss his hand were fain.
My lord the Cid spake gladly: "Now to our God on high
I make my supplication that ere I come to die I
may repay your service that house and land has cost,
And return unto you double the possession that ye lost."

My lord the Cid was merry that so great his commons grew,
And they that were come to him they all were merry too.

Six days of grace are over, and there are left but three,
Three and no more. The Cid was warned upon his guard to be,
For the King said, if thereafter he should find him in the land,
Then neither gold nor silver should redeem him from his hand.
And now the day was over and night began to fall
His cavaliers unto him he summoned one and all:

"Hearken, my noble gentlemen. And grieve not in your care.
Few goods are mine, yet I desire that each should have his share.
As good men ought, be prudent. When the cocks crow at day,
See that the steeds are saddled, nor tarry nor delay.
In San Pedro to say matins the Abbot good will be;
He will say mass in our behalf to the Holy Trinity.
And when the mass is over, from the abbey let us wend,
For the season of our sufferance draws onward to an end.
And it is sure, moreover, that we have far to go."
Since so the Cid had ordered, they must do even so.

Night passed, and came the morning. The second cock he crew;
Forthwith upon the horses the caparisons they threw.

And the bells are rung for matins with all the haste they may.
My lord Cid and his lady to church they went their way.
On the steps Xiména cast herself, that stood the shrine before,
And to God passionately she prayed to guard the Campeador:

"Our Father who art in Heaven, such glory is in Thee!
Thou madest firmament and earth, on the third day the sea.
The stars and moon Thou madest, and the great sun to warm.
In the womb of Mary Mother, Thou tookest human form.
Thou didst appear in Bethlehem as was Thy will and choice.
And in Thy praise and glory shepherds lifted up their voice.
And thither to adore Thee from Arabia afar
Came forth the three kings, Caspar, Melchior and Balthasar.
And gold and myrrh and frankincense they proffered eagerly.
Thou didst spare the prophet Jonah when he fell into the sea.
And Thou didst rescue Daniel from the lions in the cave.
And, moreover, in Rome city Saint Sebastian didst Thou save.
From the sinful lying witness Saint Susanna didst Thou ward.
And years two and thirty didst Thou walk the Earth, our Lord,
Showing, the which all men take heed, Thy miracles divine.
Of the stone, bread Thou madest, and of the water, wine.
Thou didst raise up Saint Lazarus according to Thy will.
Thou didst let the Hebrews take Thee. On Calvary the hill,
In the place Golgotha by name, Thee, Lord, they crucified.
And the two thieves were with Thee, whom they hanged on either side,
One is in heaven, the other he came not thereunto.
A miracle most mighty on the cross there didst Thou do.
Blind was Longinus never had seen from his birth-year.
The side of our Lord Jesus he pierced it with the spear.
Forth the blood issued swiftly, and ran down the shaft apace.
It stained his hands. He raised them and put them to his face.
Forthwith his eyes were opened and in every way might see.
He is ransomed from destruction for he straight believed on Thee.
From the sepulchre Thou rosest, and into Hell didst go,
According to Thy purpose, and its gates didst overthrow,
To bring forth the Holy Fathers. And King of Kings Thou art,
And of all the world the Father, and Thee with all my heart
Do I worship and acknowledge, and further I implore
That Saint Peter speed my prayer for the Cid Campeador,
That God keep his head from evil; and when this day we twain
Depart, then grant it to us that we meet in life again."

And now the prayer is over and the mass in its due course.
From church they came, and already were about to get to horse.
And the Cid clasped Xiména, but she, his hand she kissed.
Sore wept the Dame, in no way the deed to do she wist.
He turned unto his daughters and he looked upon the two:
"To the Spiritual Father, have I commended you.
We must depart. God knoweth when we shall meet again."
Weeping most sore—for never hast thou beheld such pain
As the nail from the flesh parteth, from each other did they part.

And Cid with all his vassals disposed himself to start,
And as he waited for them anew he turned his head,
Minaya Alvar Fañez then in good season said:

"Cid! Where is now thy courage? Upon a happy day
Wast thou born. Let us bethink us of the road and haste away.
A truce to this. Rejoicing out of these griefs shall grow.
The God who gave us spirits shall give us aid also."

Don Sancho the good Abbot, they charged him o'er again
To watch and ward Xiména and likewise her daughters twain,
And the ladies that were with them. That he shall have no lack
Of guerdon let the Abbot know. By this was he come back,
Then out spake Alvar Fañez: "Abbot, if it betide
That men should come desirous in our company to ride,
Bid them follow but be ready on a long road to go
Through the sown and through the desert; they may overtake us so."

They got them upon horseback, they let the rein go slack.
The time drew near when on Castile they needs must turn the back.
Spinaz de Can, it was the place where the Cid did alight.
And a great throng of people welcomed him there that night.
On the next day at morning, he got to horse once more,
And forth unto his exile rode the true Campeador.
To the left of San Estévan the good town did he wheel.
He marched through Alcobiella the frontier of Castile.
O'er the highway to Quinéa his course then has he bent.
Hard by Navas de Palos o'er Duéro stream he went.
All night at Figueruéla did my lord the Cid abide.
And very many people welcomed him on every side..

XIX.

When it was night the Cid lay down. In a deep sleep he fell,
And to him in a vision came the angel Gabriel:

"Ride, Cid, most noble Campeador, for never yet did knight
Ride forth upon an hour whose aspect was so bright.
While thou shalt live good fortune shall be with thee and shine."
When he awoke, upon his face he made the holy sign.

XX.

He crossed himself, and unto God his soul commended then,
he was glad of the vision that had come into his ken
The next day at morning they began anew to wend.
Be it known their term of sufferance at the last has made an end.
In the mountains of Miédes the Cid encamped that night,
With the towers of Atiénza where the Moors reign on the right.

XXI.

'Twas not yet come to sunset, and lingered still the day.
My lord the Cid gave orders his henchmen to array.
Apart from the footsoldiers, and valiant men of war,
There were three hundred lances that each a pennon bore.

XXII.

"Feed all the horses early, so may our God you speed.
Let him eat who will; who will not, let him get upon the steed.

We shall pass the mountain ranges rough and of dreadful height.
The land of King Alfonso we can leave behind tonight.
And whosoe'er will seek us shall find us ready then."

By night the mountain ranges he traversed with his men.
Morn came. From the hills downward they were about to fare.
In a marvelous great forest the Cid bade halt them there,
And to feed the horses early; and he told them all aright
In what way he was desirous that they should march by night.
They all were faithful vassals and gave assent thereto;
The behests of their great captain it behooved them all to do.
Ere night, was every man of them unto the riding fit.
So did the Cid that no man might perchance get wind of it.
They marched all through the night-tide and rested not at all.

Near Henáres a town standeth that Castejón men call.
There the Cid went into ambush with the men of his array.

XXIII.

He couched there in the ambush till the breaking of the day.
This Minaya Alvar Fañez had counselled and had planned:

"Ha, Cid, in happy hour thou girdedst on the brand.
Thou with an hundred henchmen shalt abide to hold the rear.
Till we have drawn forth Castejón unto the bushment here.
But give me now two hundred men on a harrying raid to ride.
We shall win much if thy fortune and our God be on our side.

"Well didst thou speak, Minaya," the Campeador he said,
"Do thou with the two hundred ride on a harrying raid.
With Alvar Salvadórez, Alvar Alvarez shall advance,
likewise Galínd Garcíaz, who is a gallant lance.
Let them ride beside Minaya, each valiant cavalier.
Let them ride unfearing forward and turn from naught for fear.
Out unto Guadalajára, from Hita far and wide,
To Alcalá the city forth let the harriers ride.
That they bring all the booty let them be very sure,
Let them leave naught behind them for terror of the Moor.
Here with an hundred lances in the rear will I remain,
And capture Castejón good store of provender to gain.
If thou come in any danger as thou ridest on the raid,
Send swiftly hither, and all Spain shall say how I gave aid."
Now all the men were chosen who on the raid should ride,
And those who in the rearguard with the lord Cid should abide.

And now the dawn was breaking and morning coming on,
And the sun rising. Very God! how beautifully it shone!
All men arose in Castejón, and wide they threw the gates;
And forth they went to oversee their farmlands and estates.
All were gone forth, and the gates stand open as they were thrown,
And but a little remnant were left in Castejón.
Round the city were the people scattered the whole country o'er.
Then forth out of the ambush issued the Campeador.
And without fail round Castejón he rushed along his way.
The Moors, both men and women, he took them for a prey,
And of their flocks as many as thereabouts there strayed.
My lord Cid don Rodrigo straight for the gateway made,
And they that held it, when they saw that swift attack begin,
Fled in great fear, and through the gates Roy Diaz entered in

With the sword naked in his hand; and fifteen Moors he slew
Whom he ran down. In Castejón much gold, and silver too,
He captured. Then unto him his knights the booty brought.
To my lord Cid they bore it. The spoil they valued naught.

Lo! the two hundred men and three to plunder that rode out,
Sped fearlessly, and ravaged the country roundabout.
For the banner of Minaya unto Alcalá did gleam.
Then they bore home the booty up the Henáres stream
Past Guadalajára. Booty exceeding great they bore
Of sheep and kine and vesture and of other wealth good store.
Straightway returned Minaya. None dared the rear attack.
With the treasure they had taken his company turned back.
Lo, they wore come to Castejón, where the Campeador abode.
He left the hold well guarded. Out from the place he rode.
With all his men about him to meet them did he come,
And with arms wide asunder welcomed Minaya home:

"Thou art come, Alvar Fañez, good lance thou art indeed.
Whereso I send thee, in such wise I well may hope to speed.
Put straightway al] together the spoil both shine and mine;
The fifth part of all, Minaya, an thou so desire, is thine."

XXIV.

"Much do I thank thee for it, illustrious Campeador.
With what thou giv'st me, the fifth part of all our spoils of war,
The King Alfonso of Castile full well content would be.
I renounce it in thy favor; and without a claim to thee.
But I swear to God who dwelleth in the high firmament,
That till upon my charger I gallop in content
Against the Moors, and till I wield both spear and brand again,
And till unto my elbow from the blade the blood doth drain
Before the Cid illustrious, howe'er so small it be,
I will not take the value of a copper groat from thee.
When through me some mighty treasure thou hast at thy command.
I will take thy gift; till such a time, all else is in thine hand."

XXV.

They heaped the spoil together. Pondered the Cid my lord,
He who in happy hour had girded on the sword,
How tidings of his raiding to the King would come ere long,
And Alfonso soon would seek him with his host to do him wrong.
He bade his spoil-dividers make a division fair,
And furthermore in writing give to each man his share.
The fortune of each cavalier had sped exceeding well,
One hundred marks of silver to each of them there fell,
And each of the foot soldiers the half of that obtained.
A round fifth of the treasure for my lord the Cid remained
But here he could not sell it, nor in gifts give it away.
No captives, men or women, he desired in his array.
And with the men of Castejón he spoke to this intent
To Hita and Guadalajára ambassadors he sent
To find how high the ransom of the fifth part they would rate.
Even as they assessed it, his profit would be great.
Three thousand marks of silver the Moors agreed to pay.
The Cid was pleased. And duly was it paid on the third day.

My lord the Cid determined with all his men of war
That there within the castle they would abide no more,
And that they would have held it, but that water sore it lacked:

"Ye Moors are friendly to the King; even so runs the pact,
With his host will he pursue us. And I desire to flee
From Castejón; Minaya and my men, so hark to me;

XXVI.

"Nor take it ill, mine utterance. For here we cannot stay.
The king will come to seek us, for he is not far away;
But to destroy the castle seems in no way good to me.
An hundred Moorish women in that place I will set free
And of the Moors an hundred. Since there, as it befell,
I captured them. Hereafter shall they all speak of me well.
Ye all are paid; among you is no man yet to pay.
Let us on the morrow morning prepare to ride away,
For against my lord Alfonso the strife I would not stir."

What the Cid said was pleasing to his every follower.
Rich men they all departed from the hold that they had ta'en
And the Moors both men and women blessed them o'er and o'er again.

Up the Henáres hastened they and hard they rode and strong.
They passed through the Alcárrias, and swift they marched along,
By the Caverns of Anquíta they hastened on their way.
They crossed the stream. Into Taránz the great plain entered they,
And on down through that region as hard as they might fare.
Twixt Faríza and Cetína would the Cid seek shelter there.
And a great spoil he captured in the country as he went,
For the Moors had no inkling whatso'er of his intent.
On the next day marched onward the great Cid of Bivár,
And he went by Alháma, and down the vale afar.
And he passed Bubiérca and Atéca likewise passed,
And it was nigh to Alcocér that he would camp at last
Upon a rounded hillock that was both strong and high.
They could not rob him of water; the Jalón it flowed hard by.
My lord Cid don Rodrigo planned to storm Alcocér.

XXVII.

He pitched a strong encampment upon the hillock there,
Some men were toward the mountains, some by the stream arrayed.
The gallant Cid, who in good hour had girded on the blade,
Bade his men near the water dig a trench about the height,
That no man might surprise them by day nor yet by night.
So might men know that there the Cid had taken up his stand.

XXVIII.

And thereupon the tidings went out through all that land,
How my lord Cid the Campeador had there got footing sure,
He is gone forth from the Christians, he is come unto the Moor,
In his presence no man dareth plough the farmlands as of yore.
Very merry with his vassals was the great Campeador.
And Alcocér the Castle wider tribute had he laid.

XXIX.

In Alcocér the burghers to the Cid their tribute paid
And all the dwellers in Terrér and Teca furthermore.
And the townsmen of Calatayúd, know well, it irked them sore.
Full fifteen weeks he tarried there, but the town yielded not.
And when he saw it forthwith the Cid devised a plot.
Save one left pitched behind him, he struck his every tent.
Then with his ensign lifted, down the Jalón he went,
With mail-shirts on and girded swords, as a wise man should him bear.
To draw forth to his ambush the men of Alcocér.

And when they saw it, name of God! How glad was everyone!
"The provender and fodder of my lord the Cid are gone.
If he leaves one tent behind him, the burden is not light
Of the others that he beareth. He 'scapes like one in flight.
Let us now fall upon him, great profit shall we gain.
We shall win a mighty booty before he shall be ta'en
By them who have their dwelling in the city of Terrér;
For if by chance they take him, in the spoil we shall not share.
The tribute that he levied, double he shall restore."

Forth from the town of Alcocér in wild haste did they pour.
When the Cid saw them well without he made as if he fled;
With his whole host in confusion down the Jalón he sped.

"The prize 'scapes," cried the townsmen. Forth rushed both great and
     small,
In the lust of conquest thinking of nothing else at all.
They left the gates unguarded, none watched them any more.
And then his face upon them turned the great Campeador,
He saw how twixt them and their hold there lay a mighty space;
He made them turn the standard. They spurred the steeds apace.
"Ho! cavaliers! Now swiftly let every man strike in,
By the Creator's favor this battle we shall win."
And there they gave them battle in the midmost of the mead.
Ah God! is the rejoicing on this morning great indeed.
The Cid and Alvar Fañez went spurring on ahead;
Know ye they had good horses that to their liking sped.
'Twixt the townsmen and the castle swiftly the way they broke.
And the Cid's henchmen merciless, came striking stroke on stroke,
In little space three hundred of the Moors they there have slain.
Loud was the shouting of the Moors in the ambush that were ta'en.
But the twain left them; on they rushed. Right for the hold they made
And at the gate they halted, each with a naked blade.
Then up came the Cid's henchmen for the foe were all in flight.
Know ye the Cid has taken Alcocér by such a sleight.

XXX.

Per Vermudóz came thither who the Cid's flag did bear.
On the high place of the city he lifted it in air.
Outspoke the Cid Roy Diaz. Born in good hour was he:

"To God in Heaven and all his saints great thanks and praises be.
We shall better now our lodging for cavalier and steed."

XXXI.

Alvar Fañez and all ye my knights, now hearken and give heed
We have taken with the castle a booty manifold.
Dead are the Moors. Not many of the living I behold.
Surely we cannot sell them the women and the men;
And as for striking off their heads, we shall gain nothing then.
In the hold let us receive them, for we have the upper hand.
When we lodge within their dwellings, they shall do as we command."

XXXII.

The Cid with all his booty lieth in Alcocér.
He let the tent be sent for, that he left behind him there.
It irked the men of Teca, wroth in Terrér were they;
Know ye on all Calatayúd sorely the thing did weigh.
To the Sovereign of Valencia they sent the news apace:
How that the King Alfonso hath banished in disgrace
One whom men call my lord the Cid, Roy Diaz of Bivár,
He came to lodge by Alcocér, and strong his lodgings are.
He drew them out to ambush; he has won the castle there.
"If thou aidest not needs must thou lose both Teca and Terrér,
Thou wilt have lost Calatayúd that cannot stand alone.
All things will go to ruin on the banks of the Jalón,
And round about Jilóca on the far bank furthermore."

When the King Tamín had heard it, his heart was troubled sore:
"Here do I see three Moorish kings. Let two without delay
With three thousand Moors and weapons for the fight ride there away;
Likewise they shall be aided by the men of the frontier.
See that ye take him living and bring him to me here.
He must pay for the realm's trespass till I be satisfied."

Three thousand Moors have mounted and fettled them to ride.
All they unto Segórbe have come to lodge that night.
The next day they got ready to ride at morning light.
In the evening unto Celfa they came the night to spend.
And there they have determined for the borderers to send.
Little enow they tarried; from every side they came.
Then they went forth from Celfa (of Canál it has its name),
Never a whit they rested, but marched the livelong day.
And that night unto their lodging in Calatayúd came they.
And they sent forth their heralds through the length of all the land.
A great and sovran army they gathered to their hand.
With the two Kings Fáriz and Gálve (these are the names they bear).

They will besiege my noble lord the Cid in Alcocér.

XXXIII.

They pitched the tents and got them to their lodging there and then.
Strong grew their bands for thereabouts was found great store of men.
Moreover all the outposts, which the Moors set in array,
Marched ever hither and thither in armour night and day.
And many are the outposts, and great that host of war.
From the Cid's men, of water have they cut off all the store.
My lord the Cid's brave squadrons great lust to fight they had,
But he who in good hour was born firmly the thing forbade.
For full three weeks together they hemmed the city in.

XXXIV.

When three weeks were well nigh over and the fourth would soon begin,
My lord Cid and his henchmen agreed after this guise:

"They have cut us off from water; and our food must fail likewise.
They will not grant unto us that we depart by night,
And very great is their power for us to face and fight.
My knights what is your pleasure, now say, that we shall do.?
Then first outspake Minaya the good knight and the true:

"Forth from Castile the noble unto this place we sped;
If with the Moors we fight not, they will not give us bread.
Here are a good six hundred and some few more beside.
In the name of the Creator let nothing else betide:
Let us smite on them tomorrow."

The Campeador said he:
"Minaya Alvar Fañez, thy speaking liketh me.
Thou hast done thyself much honor, as of great need thou must."

All the Moors, men and women, he bade them forth to thrust
That none his secret counsel might understand aright
And thereupon they armed them all through that day and night.
And the next day in the dawning when soon the sun should rise,
The Cid was armed and with him all the men of his emprise.
My lord the Cid spake to them even as you shall hear.

"Let all go forth, let no one here tarry in the rear,
Save only two footsoldiers the gates to watch and shield.
They will capture this our castle, if we perish in the field;

But if we win, our fortunes shall grow both great and fair.
Per Vermudóz, my banner I bid thee now to bear;
As thou art very gallant, do thou keep it without stain.
But unless I so shall order thou shalt not loose the rein."

He kissed the Cid's hand. Forth he ran the battle-flag to take.
They oped the gates, and outward in a great rush did they break.
And all the outposts of the Moor beheld them coming on,
And back unto the army forthwith they got them gone.
What haste there was among the Moors! To arm they turned them back.
With the thunder of the war-drum the earth was like to crack.
There might you see Moors arming, that swift their ranks did close.
Above the Moorish battle two flags-in-chief arose,
But of their mingling pennons the number who shall name?
Now all the squadrons of the Moors marching right onward came,
That the Cid and all his henchmen they might capture out of hand.

"My gallant men here in this place see that ye firmly stand,
Let no man leave the war-ranks till mine order I declare."

Per Vermudóz, he found it too hard a thing to bear,
He spurred forth with the banner that in his hand he bore:

"May the Creator aid thee, thou true Cid Campeador,
Through the line of battle yonder thy standard I will take;
I shall see how you bring succor, who must for honor's sake."
Said the Campeador: "Of charity, go not to the attack."
For answer said Per Vermudóz: "Is naught shall hold me back."
Spurring the steed he hurled him through the strong line of the foes.
The serried Moors received him and smote him mighty blows,
To take from him the banner; yet they could not pierce his mail.
Said the Campeador: "Of charity go help him to prevail."

XXXV.

Before their breasts the war-shields there have they buckled strong,
The lances with the pennons they laid them low along,
And they have bowed their faces over the saddlebow,
And thereaway to strike them with brave hearts did they go.
He who in happy hour was born with a great voice did call:

"For the love of the Creator, smite them, my gallants ah.
I am Roy Diaz of Bivár, the Cid, the Campeador."

At the rank where was Per Vermudóz the mighty strokes they bore.

They are three hundred lances that each a pennon bear.
At one blow every man of them his Moor has slaughtered there,
And when they wheeled to charge anew as many more were slain.

XXXV.

You might see great clumps of lances lowered and raised again,
And many a shield of leather pierced and shattered by the stroke,
And many a coat of mail run through, its meshes all to-broke,
And many a white pennon come forth all red with blood,
And running without master full many a charger good.

Cried the Moors "Mahound!" The Christians shouted on Saint James of
  grace.
On the field Moors thirteen hundred were slain in little space.

XXXVII.

On his gilded selle how strongly fought the Cid, the splendid knight.
And Minaya Alvar Fañez who Zoríta held of right,
And brave Martin Antolínez that in Burgos did abide,
And likewise Muño Gustióz, the Cid's esquire tried!
So also Martin Gustióz who ruled Montemayór,
And by Alvar Salvadórez Alvar Alvarez made war
And Galínd Garcíaz the good knight that came from Aragon,
There too came Felez Múñoz the Cid his brother's son.
As many as were gathered there straightway their succor bore,
And they sustained the standard and the Cid Campeador.

XXXVIII.

Of Minaya Alvar Fañez the charger they have slain
The gallant bands of Christians came to his aid amain.
His lance was split and straightway he set hand upon the glaive,
What though afoot, no whit the less he dealt the buffets brave.
The Cid, Roy Diaz of Castile, saw how the matter stood.
He hastened to a governor that rode a charger good.
With his right hand he smote him such a great stroke with the sword
That the waist he clave; the half of him he hurled unto the sward.
To Minaya Alvar Fañez forthwith he gave the steed.
"Right arm of mine, Minaya, now horse thee with all speed!
I shall have mighty succor from thee this very day.

The Moors leave not the battle; firm standeth their array,
And surely it behooves us to storm their line once more."

Sword in hand rode Minaya; on their host he made great war,
Whom he overtook soever, even to death he did.
He who was born in happy hour, Roy Diaz, my lord Cid,
Thrice smote against King Fáriz. Twice did the great strokes fail,
But the third found the quarry. And down his shirt of mail
Streamed the red blood. To leave the field he wheeled his horse away.
By that one stroke the foeman were conquered in the fray.

XXXIX.

And Martin Antolínez a heavy stroke let drive
At Gálve. On his helmet the rubies did he rive;
The stroke went through the helmet for it reached unto the flesh.
Be it known, he dared not tarry for the man to strike afresh.
King Fáriz and King Gálve, but beaten men are they.
What a great day for Christendom! On every side away
Fled the Moors. My lord Cid's henchmen still striking gave them chase.
Into Terrér came Fáriz, but the people of the place
Would not receive King Gálve. As swiftly as he might
Onward unto Calatayúd he hastened in his flight.
And after him in full pursuit came on the Campeador.
Till they came unto Calatayúd that chase they gave not o'er.

XL.

Minaya Alvar Fañez hath a horse that gallops well.
Of the Moors four and thirty that day before him fell.
And all his arm was bloody, for 'tis a biting sword;
And streaming from his elbow downward the red blood poured.
Said Minaya: "Now am I content; well will the rumor run
To Castile, for a pitched battle my lord the Cid hath won."
Few Moors are left, so many have already fallen dead,
For they who followed after slew them swiftly as they fled.
He who was born in happy hour came with his host once more.
On his noble battle-charger rode the great Campeador.
His coif was wrinkled. Name of God! but his great beard was fair.
His mail-hood on his shoulders lay. His sword in hand he bare.
And he looked upon his henchmen and saw them drawing nigh:

"Since we ha' won such a battle, glory to God on high!"

The Cid his henchmen plundered the encampment far and wide
Of the shields and of the weapons and other wealth beside.

Of the Moors they captured there were found five hundred steeds and
  ten.
And there was great rejoicing among those Christian men,
And the lost of their number were but fifteen all told.
They brought a countless treasure of silver and of gold.
Enriched were all those Christians with the spoil that they had ta'en
And back unto their castle they restored the Moors again;
To give them something further he gave command and bade.
With all his train of henchmen the Cid was passing glad.
He gave some monies, some much goods to be divided fair,
And full an hundred horses fell to the Cid's fifth share.
God's name! his every vassal nobly did he requite,
Not only the footsoldiers but likewise every knight.
He who in happy hour was born wrought well his government,
And all whom he brought with him therewith were well content.

"Harken to me, Minaya, my own right arm art thou.
Of the wealth, wherewith our army the Creator did endow,
Take in thine hand whatever thou deemest good to choose.
To Castile I fain would send thee to carry there the news
Of our triumph. To Alphonso the King who banished me
A gift of thirty horses I desire to send with thee.
Saddled is every charger, each steed is bridled well.
There hangeth a good war-sword at the pommel of each selle."
Said Minaya Alvar Fañez: "I will do it with good cheer.

XLI.

"Of the gold and the fine silver, behold a bootful here.
Nothing thereto is lacking. Thou shalt pay the money down
At Saint Mary's Church for masses fifty score in Burgos town;
To my wife and to my daughters the remainder do thou bear.
Let them offer day and night for me continually their prayer.
If I live, exceeding wealthy all of those dames shall be.

XLII.

Minaya Alvar Fañez, therewith content was he.
They made a choice of henchmen along with him to ride.
They fed the steeds. Already came on the eventide.
Roy Diaz would decide it with his companions leal.

XLIII.

"Dost thou then go, Minaya, to the great land of Castile

And unto our well-wishers with a clear heart canst thou say:
'God granted us his favor, and we conquered in the fray?'
If returning thou shalt find us here in this place, 'tis well;
If not, where thou shalt hear of us, go seek us where we dwell.
For we must gain our daily bread with the lance and with the brand,
Since otherwise we perish here in a barren land.
And therefore as methinketh, we must get hence away."

XLIV.

So was it, and Minaya went at the break of day.
But there behind the Campeador abode with all his band.
And waste was all the country, an exceeding barren land.
Each day upon my lord the Cid there in that place they spied,
The Moors that dwelt on the frontier and outlanders beside.
Healed was King Fáriz. With him they held a council there,
The folk that dwelt in Teca and the townsmen of Terrér,
And the people of Calatayúd, of the three the fairest town.
In such wise have they valued it and on parchment set it down
That for silver marks three thousand Alcocér the Cid did sell.

XLV.

Roy Diaz sold them Alcocér. How excellently well
He paid his vassals! Horse and foot he made them wealthy then,
And a poor man you could not find in all his host of men.
In joy he dwelleth aye who serves a lord of noble heart.

XLVI.

When my lord the Cid was ready from the Castle to depart,
The Moors both men and women cried out in bitter woe:
"Lord Cid art thou departing? Still may our prayers go
Before thy path, for with thee we are full well content."
For my lord the great Cid of Bivár, when from Alcocér he went,
The Moors both men and women made lamentation sore.
He lifted up the standard, forth marched the Campeador.
Down the Jalón he hastened, on he went spurring fast.
He saw birds of happy omen, as from the stream he passed.
Glad were the townsmen of Terrér that he had marched away,
And the dwellers in Calatayúd were better pleased than they.
But in the town of Alcocér 'twas grief to all and one,
For many a deed of mercy unto them the Cid had done.
My lord the Cid spurred onward. Forward apace he went;
'Twas near to the hill Monreál that he let pitch his tent.

Great is the hill and wondrous and very high likewise.
Be it known from no quarter doth he need to dread surprise.
And first he forced Doróca tribute to him to pay,
And then levied on Molína on the other side that lay,
Teruél o'er against him to submit he next compelled
And lastly Celfa de Canál within his power he held.

XLVII.

May my lord the Cid, Roy Diaz, at all times God's favor feel.
Minaya Alvar Fañez has departed to Castile.
To the King thirty horses for a present did he bring.
And when he had beheld them beautifully smiled the King:
"Who gave thee these, Minaya, so prosper thee the Lord?"
"Even the Cid Roy Diaz, who in good hour girded sword.
Since you banished him, by cunning has he taken Alcocér.
To the King of Valencia the tidings did they bear.
He bade that they besiege him; from every water-well
They cut him off. He sallied forth from the citadel,
In the open field he fought them, and he beat in that affray
Two Moorish kings he captured, sire, a very mighty prey.
Great King, this gift he sends thee. Thine hands and feet also
He kisses. Show him mercy; such God to thee shall show."
Said the King:
"'Tis over early for one banished, without grace
In his lord's sight, to receive it at the end of three week's space.
But since 'tis Moorish plunder to take it I consent.
That the Cid has taken such a spoil, I am full well content.
Beyond all this. Minaya. thine exemption I accord,
For all thy lands and honors are unto thee restored.
Go and come! Henceforth my favor I grant to thee once more.
But to thee I say nothing of the Cid Campeador.

XLVIII.

"Beyond this, Alvar Fañez, I am fain to tell it thee
That whosoever in my realm in that desire may be,
Let them, the brave and gallant, to the Cid betake them straight.
I free them and exempt them both body and estate."
Minaya Alvar Fañez has kissed the King's hands twain:

"Great thanks, as to my rightful lord I give thee, King, again.
This dost thou now, and better yet as at some later hour.
We shall labor to deserve it, if God will give us power."
Said the King: "Minaya, peace for that. Take through Castile thy way.

None shall molest. My lord the Cid seek forth without delay."

XLIX.

Of him I fain would tell you in good hour that girt the blade.
The hill, where his encampment in that season he had made,
While the Moorish folk endureth, while there are Christians still,
Shall they ever name in writing 'My Lord the Cid, his Hill.'
While he was there great ravage in all the land he made,
Under tribute the whole valley of the Martin he laid.
And unto Zaragoza did the tidings of him go,
Nor pleased the Moors; nay rather they were filled with grievous woe.
For fifteen weeks together my lord Cid there did stay.
When the good knight saw how greatly Minaya did delay,
Then forth with all his henchmen on a night march he tried.
And he left all behind him, and forsook the mountain side,
Beyond the town of Teruél good don Rodrigo went.
In the pine grove of Tévar Roy Diaz pitched his tent.
And all the lands about him he harried in the raid,
And on Zaragoza city a heavy tribute laid.

When this he had accomplished and three weeks had made an end,
Out of Castile Minaya unto the Cid did wend.
Two hundred knights were with him that had belted on the brands.
Know ye well that there were many foot-soldiers in his bands.
When the Cid saw Minaya draw near unto his view,
With his horse at a full gallop to embrace the man he flew.
He kissed his mouth, his very eyes in that hour kissed the Cid.
And then all things he told him, for naught from him he hid.
Then beautifully upon him smiled the good Campeador:
"God and his righteousness divine be greatly praised therefor.
While thou shalt live, Minaya, well goeth this my game."

L.

God! How happy was the army that thus Minaya came,
For of them they left behind them he brought the tidings in,
From comrade and from brethren and the foremost of their kin.

LI.

But God! What a glad aspect the Cid fair-bearded wore
That duly had Minaya paid for masses fifty score,
And of his wife and daughters all of the state displayed!
God! How content was he thereat! What noble cheer he made!

"Ha! Alvar Fañez, many now may thy life-days be.
What fair despatch thou madest! Thou art worth more than we."

LII.

And he who in good hour was born tarried in no way then,
But he took knights two hundred, and all were chosen men;
And forth when fell the evening a-raiding did they haste.
At Alcañiz the meadows the Campeador laid waste,
And gave all places round about to ravage and to sack.
On the third day to whence he came the Cid again turned back.

LIII.

Thro' all the country roundabout have the tidings of them flown.
It grieved the men of Huésca and the people of Monzón.
Glad were they in Zaragoza since the tribute they had paid,
For outrage at Roy Diaz's hand no whit were they afraid.

LIV.

Then back to their encampment they hastened with their prey.
All men were very merry for a mighty spoil had they.
The Cid was glad exceeding; Alvar Fañez liked it well.
But the great Cid smiled, for there at ease he could not bear to dwell.

"Ha! All my knights, unto you the truth will I confess:
Who still in one place tarries, his fortune will grow less.
Let us tomorrow morning prepare to ride apace,
Let us march and leave forever our encampment in this place."
Unto the pass of Alucát the lord Cid got him gone.
Then to Huésca and to Montalban he hastily marched on.
And ten full days together on that raid they were to ride.
The tidings to all quarters went flying far and wide,
how that the Exile from Castile great harm to them had done.

LV.

Afar into all quarters did the tidings of him run.
They brought the message to the Count of Barcelona's hand,
How that the Cid Roy Diaz was o'errunning all the land.
He was wroth. For a sore insult the tiding did he take.

LVI.

The Count was a great braggart and an empty word he spake:
"Great wrongs he put upon me, he of Bivár, the Cid.
Within my very palace much shame to me he did:
He gave no satisfaction though he struck my brother's son;
And the lands in my keeping now doth he over-run.
I challenged him not; our pact of peace I did not overthrow;
But since he seeks it of me, to demand it I will go."

He gathered the his powers that were exceeding strong,
Great bands of Moors and Christians to his array did throng.
After the lord Cid of Bivár they went upon their way,
Three nights and days together upon the march were they.
At length in Tévar's pine grove the Cid they have o'erta'en.
So strong were they that captive to take him were they fain.

My lord Cid don Rodrigo bearing great spoil he went.
From the ridge unto the valley he had finished the descent.
And in that place they bore him Count don Remónd his word.
My lord Cid sent unto him when the message he had heard:

"Say to the Count that it were well his anger now should cease.
No goods of his I carry. Let him leave me in peace."

Thereto the Count gave answer: "Not so the matter ends.
For what was and is of evil he shall make me full amends.
The Exile shall know swiftly whom he has sought to slight."

Back hastened the ambassador as swiftly as he might.
And then my lord Cid of Bivár knew how the matter lay,
And that without a battle they could not get away.

LVII.

"Ha! lay aside your booty now, every cavalier,
And take in hand your weapons, and get on your battle-gear.
Count don Remónd against us will deliver battle strong;
Great bands of Moors and Christians he brings with him along.
He will not for any reason without fighting let us go.
Here let us have the battle since they pursue us so.
So get you on your armour and girth the horses tight.
Down the hill they come in hosen and their saddles are but light,
And loose their girths. Each man of us has a Galician selle,
And moreover with the jackboots are our hosen covered well.

We should beat them though we numbered but fivescore cavaliers.
Before they reach the level, let us front them with the spears.
For each you strike three saddles thereby shall empty go.
Who was the man he hunted, Remónd Berenguél shall know
This day in Tévar's pine grove, who would take from me my prey."

LVIII.

When thus the Cid had spoken, were all in good array;
They had taken up their weapons and each had got to horse.
They beheld the Frankish army down the hill that held its course.
And at the end of the descent, close to the level land,
The Cid who in good hour was born, to charge them gave command.
And this did his good henchmen perform with all their heart;
With the pennons and the lances they nobly played their part,
Smiting at some, and others overthrowing in their might.
He who was born in happy hour has conquered in the fight.
There the Count don Remónd he took a prisoner of war,
And Coláda the war-falchion worth a thousand marks and more.

LIX.

By the victory there much honor unto his beard he did.
And then the Count to his own tent was taken by the Cid.
He bade his squires guard him. From the tent he hastened then.
From every side together about him came his men.
The Cid was glad, so mighty were the spoils of that defeat.
For the lord Cid don Rodrigo they prepared great stock of meat.
But namely the Count don Remónd, thereby he set no store.
To him they brought the viands, and placed them him before.
He would not eat, and at them all he mocked with might and main:

"I will not eat a mouthful for all the wealth in Spain;
Rather will I lose my body and forsake my soul forby,
Since beaten in the battle by such tattered louts was I."

LX.

My lord the Cid Roy Diaz you shall hearken what he said:
"Drink of the wine I prithee, Count, eat also of the bread.
If this thou dost, no longer shalt thou be a captive then;
If not, then shalt thou never see Christendom again."

LXI.

"Do thou eat, don Rodrigo, and prepare to slumber sweet.
For myself I will let perish, and nothing will I eat."
And in no way were they able to prevail till the third day,
Nor make him eat a mouthful while they portioned the great prey.

LXII.

"Ho! Count, do thou eat somewhat," even so my lord Cid spoke,
"If thou dost not eat, thou shalt not look again on Christian folk;
If in such guise thou eatest that my will is satisfied,
Thyself, Count, and, moreover, two noblemen beside
Will I make free of your persons and set at liberty."

And when the Count had heard it exceeding glad was he.
"Cid, if thou shalt perform it, this promise thou dost give,
Thereat I much shall marvel as long as I shall live."
"Eat then, oh Count; when fairly thy dinner thou hast ta'en
I will then set at liberty thee and the other twain.
But what in open battle thou didst lose and I did earn,
Know that not one poor farthing's worth to thee will I return,
For I need it for these henchmen who hapless follow me.
They shall be paid with what I win from others as from thee.
With the Holy Father's favor we shall live after this wise,
Like banished men who have not any grace in the King's eyes."

Glad was the Count. For water he asked his hands to lave.
And that they brought before him, and quickly to him gave.
The Count of Barcelona began to eat his fill
With the men the Cid had given him, and God! with what a will!
He who in happy hour was born unto the Count sate near:

"Ha! Count, if now thou dinest not with excellent good cheer,
And to my satisfaction, here we shall still delay,
And we twain in no manner shall go forth hence away."
Then said the Count: "Right gladly and according to my mind! "
With his two knights at that season in mighty haste he dined.
My lord the Cid was well content that all his eating eyed,
For the Count don Remónd his hands exceeding nimbly plied.

"If thou art pleased, my lord the Cid, in guise to go are we.
Bid them bring to us our horses; we will mount speedily.
Since I was first Count, never have I dined with will so glad,
Nor shall it be forgotten what joy therein I had."

They gave to them three palfreys. Each had a noble selle.
Good robes of fur they gave them, and mantles fair as well.
Count don Remónd rode onward with a knight on either side.
To the camp's end the Castilian along with them did ride.

"Ha! Count, forth thou departest to freedom fair and frank;
For what thou hast left with me I have thee now to thank.
If desire to avenge it is present to thy mind,
Send unto me beforehand when thou comest me to find.
Either that thou wilt leave thy goods or part of mine wilt seize."

"Ha! my lord Cid, thou art secure, be wholly at thine ease.
Enough have I paid to thee till all this year be gone.
As for coming out to find thee, I will not think thereon."

LXIII.

The Count of Barcelona spurred forth. Good speed he made.
Turning his head he looked at them, for he was much afraid
Lest my lord the Cid repent him; the which the gallant Cid
Would not have done for all the world. Base deed he never did.
The Count is gone. He of Bivár has turned him back again;
He began to be right merry, and he mingled with his train.
Most great and wondrous was the spoil that they had won in war,
So rich were his companions that they knew not what they bore.

CANTAR II

THE MARRIAGE OF THE CID'S DAUGHTERS

LXIV.

Here of my lord Cid of Bivár begins anew the Song.
Within the pass of Alucát my lord Cid made him strong,
He has left Zaragoza and the lands that near it lie,
And all the coasts of Montalban and Huésca he passed by,
And unto the salt ocean he began the way to force.
In the East the sun arises; thither he turned his course.
On Jérica and Almenár and Onda he laid hand,
Round about Bórriana he conquered all the land.

LXV.

God helped him, the Creator in Heaven that doth dwell
Beside these Murviédro hath the Cid ta'en as well.
Then that the Lord was on his side, the Cid beheld it clear.
In the city of Valencia arose no little fear.

LXVI.

It irked them in Valencia. It gave them no delight,
Be it known; that to surround him they planned. They marched by night
They pulled up at Murviédro to camp as morning broke.
My lord the Cid beheld it and wondering much he spoke:
"Father in Heaven, mighty thanks must I now proffer Thee.
In their lands we dwell and do them every sort of injury;
And we have drunk their liquor, of their bread our meal we make.
If they come forth to surround us, justly they undertake.
Without a fight this matter will in no way be a-paid.
Let messengers go seek them who now should bear us aid;
Let them go to them in Jérica and Alucát that are
And thence to Onda. Likewise let them go to Almenár.
Let the men of Bórriana hither at once come in.
In this place a pitched battle we shall certainly begin.
I trust much will be added to our gain in this essay."

They all were come together in his host on the third day.
And he who in good hour was born 'gan speak his meaning clear:

"So may the Creator aid us, my gallants hark and hear.
Since we have left fair Christendom—We did not as we would;

We could no other—God be praised our fortune has been good.
The Valencians besiege us. If here we would remain,
They must learn of us a lesson excelling in its pain.

LXVII.

"Let the night pass and morning come. Look that ye ready be
With arms and horses. We will forth that host of theirs to see.'.
Like men gone out in exile into a strange empire,
There shall it be determined who is worthy of his hire."

VIII.

Minaya Alvar Fañez, hark what he said thereto:
"Ho! Campeador, thy pleasure in all things may we do.
Give me of knights an hundred, I ask not one other man.
And do thou with the others smite on them in the van
While my hundred storm their rearward, upon them thou shalt thrust—
Ne'er doubt it. We shall triumph as in God is all my trust."
Whatsoever he had spoken filled the Cid with right good cheer

And now was come the morning, and they donned their battle gear.
What was his task of battle every man of them did know.
At the bleak of day against them forth did the lord Cid go.
"In God's name and Saint James', my knights, strike hard into the war,
And manful. The lord Cid am I, Roy Diaz of Bivár!"

You might see a many tent-ropes everywhither broken lie,
And pegs wrenched up; the tent-posts on all sides leaned awry.
The Moors were very many. To recover they were fain,
But now did Alvar Fañez on their rearward fall amain.
Though bitterly it grieved them, they had to fly and yield.
Who could put trust in horsehoofs, and forthwith fled the field.
Two kings of the Moriscos there in the rout they slew;
And even to Valencia the chase did they pursue.
And mighty is the booty my lord the Cid had ta 'en.
They ravaged all the country and then turned back again.
They brought to Murviédro the booty of the foes.
And great was the rejoicing in the city that arose.
Cebólla have they taken and all the lands anear.
In Valencia they knew not what to do for very fear.
Of my lord Cid the great tidings, be it known, on all sides spread.

42

LXIX.

His renown afar is spreading. Beyond the sea it sped.
Glad were the companies the Cid a glad man was he
That God had given him succor and gained that victory.
And they sent forth their harriers. By night they marched away,
They reached unto Culléra, and to Játiva came they.
And ever downward even to Dénia town they bore.
And all the Moorish country by the sea he wasted sore.
Peñacadéll, outgoing and entrance, have they ta'en.

LXX.

When the Cid took Peñacadéll, it was great grief and pain
To them who in Culléra and in Játiva did dwell,
And sorrow without measure in Valencia befell.

LXXI.

Three years those towns to conquer in the Moorish land he bode,
Winning much; by day he rested, and at night was on the road.

LXXII.

On the dwellers in Valencia they wrought chastisement sore,
From the town they dared not sally against him to make war.
He harried all their gardens and a mighty ruin made;
And all those years their harvest in utter waste he laid.
Loud lamented the Valencians, for sore bested they were,
Nor could find in any quarter any sort of provender;
Nor could the father aid the son, nor the son aid the sire,
Nor comrade comfort comrade. Gentles, 'tis hardship dire
To lack for bread, and see our wives and children waste away.
They saw their own affliction and no hope of help had they.

To the King of Morocco had they sent the tidings on.
'Gainst the lord of Montes Claros on a great war was he gone.
He counselled not. He came not to aid them in the war.

My lord the Cid had heard it. His heart was glad therefor;
And forth from Murviédro he marched away by night.
He was in the fields of Monreál at the breaking of the light.
Through Aragon the tidings he published, and Navarre,
And through the Marches of Castile he spread the news afar:

Who poverty would put away and riches would attain,
Let him seek the Cid, whoever of a soldier's life is fain.
Valencia to beleaguer he desireth to go down,
That he may unto the Christians deliver up the town

LXXIII.

"Valencia to beleaguer, who fain would march with me
Let none come hither to me, if his choice be not free.
Is nought that may compel him along with me to fare—
Canál de Celfa for three days I will tarry for him there."

LXXIV.

So my lord Cid hath spoken, the loyal Campeador.
He turned back to Murviedo that he had ta'en in war.
Be it known into all quarters went the word forth. None were fain
To delay who smelt the plunder. Crowds thronged to him amain,
Good christened folk, and ringing went his tidings far and wide;
And more men came unto him than departed from his side.
He of Bivár, my lord the Cid, great growth of riches had.
When he saw the bands assembled, he began to be right glad.
My lord Cid, don Rodrigo, for nothing would delay.
He marched against Valencia and smote on it straightway.
Well did the Cid surround it; till the leaguer closed about.
He thwarted their incomings, he checked their goings out.
To seek for alien succor he gave them time of grace;
And nine full months together he sat down before the place,
And when the tenth was coming, to yield it were they fain.

And great was the rejoicing in the city that did reign,
When the lord Cid took Valencia and within the town had won.
All of his men were cavaliers that erst afoot had gone.
Who the worth of gold and silver for your pleasure could declare?
They all were rich together as many as were there.
For himself the Cid Rodrigo took the fifth part of all,
And coined marks thirty thousand unto his share did fall.
Who could tell the other treasure? Great joy the Cid befell
And his men, when the flag-royal tossed o'er the citadel.

LXXV.

The Cid and his companions they rested in the place
Unto the King of Seville the tiding came apace:
Ta'en is Valencia city; for him 'tis held no more.

With thirty thousand armed men he came to look them o'er.
Nigh to the plain a battle they pitched both stiff and strong.
But the lord Cid long-bearded hath overthrown that throng.
And even unto Játiva in a long rout they poured.
You might have seen all bedlam on the Jucar by the ford,
For there the Moors drank water but sore against their will.
With bet thee strokes upon him 'scaped the Sovereign of Seville.
And then with all that booty the Cid came home again.
Great was Valencia's plunder what time the town was ta'en,
But that the spoils of that affray were greater yet, know well.
An hundred marks of silver to each common soldier fell.
How had shed that noble's fortune now lightly may you guess.

LXXVI.

There was among those Christians excelling happiness
For my lord Roy Diaz that was born in a season of good grace.
And now his beard was growing; longer it grew apace.
For this the Cid had spoken, this from his mouth said he,
"By my love for King Alphonso the king who banished me,"
That the shears should not shear it, nor a single hair dispart,
That so the Moors and Christians might ponder it at heart.

And resting in Valencia did the lord Cid abide,
With Minaya Alvar Fañez who would not leave his side.
They who went forth to exile of riches had good store.
To all men in Valencia, the gallant Campeador
Gave houses and possessions whereof they were right glad.
All men of the Cid's bounty good testimony had.
And of them that had come later well content was every one.
My lord Cid saw it plainly that they fain would get them gone,
With the goods that they had taken, if unhindered they might go.
The lord Cid gave his order (Minaya counselled so)
That if any man that with him in richer case did stand
Should take his leave in secret and fail to kiss his hand,
If they might overtake him and catch him as he fled,
They would seize his goods and bring him unto the gallows-head.
Lo! was it well looked after. Counsel he took again
With Minaya Alvar Fañez "An it be that thou art fain,
Gladly would I know, Minaya, what may the number be
Of my henchmen, as at present, that have gained aught by me.
I shall set it down in writing. Let them well the number scan,
Lest one depart in secret and I should miss the man.
To me and my companions his goods shall be restored,

All they who guard Valencia and keep the outer ward.

"The measure is well counselled," said Minaya therewithal.

LXXVII.

He bade them meet together at the palace, in the hall.
When he found them met together he had them numbered o'er.
Bivár's great Cid had with him thousands three, and thirty score.
His heart was glad within him, and a smile was on his face.
"Thanks be to God, Minaya, and to Mary Mother's grace.
Out from Bivár the city we led a lesser power.
Wealth have we, and shall have greater as at some later hour.

"Minaya, if it please thee, if it seemeth good to thee,
To Castile I fain would send thee, where our possessions be,
Unto the King Alphonso that is my lord by right.
Out of the mighty plunder we won here in the fight
I would give him five score horses, the which to him now take;
kiss thou his hand and earnestly plead with him for the sake
Of my wife Xiména and the twain, maids of my blood that be,
If yet it be his pleasure that they be brought to me.

I will send for them. But be it known how this my message runs:
The lady of my lord the Cid and her maids, my little ones,
Men shall seek for in such fashion that
They shall come to the strange country we have conquered by our
   might."

To him Minaya answered: "Yea and with right good heart."
After they thus had spoken they got ready to depart.
The Cid to Alvar Fañez an hundred men decreed
To do his will, and serve him on the journey at his need.
And he bade give to San Pedro marks of silver fifty score,
And beside to Abbot Sancho a full five hundred morn

LXXVIII.

Of these things while they were joyous, came thither from the East,
A clerk, the Bishop don Jerome, so all men called that priest.
Excelling was his knowledge, and prudent was his rede,
'Twas a mighty man of valor afoot or on the steed.
Of the Cid's deeds the tidings he was seeking to procure,
And he yearned sore, ever sighing for battle with the Moor.
If his fill of fight and wounding with his hands he e'er should get,

Therefore a Christian never need have reason for regret.
When my lord the Cid had heard it, he was well pleased thereby:

"Hark, Minaya Alvar Fañez, by him who is on high,
When the Lord God would aid us, let us give Him thanks again. .
Round Valencia a bishopric to stablish I am fain,
And I will further give it unto this Christian leal.
Thou shalt bear with thee good tidings when thou goest to Castile."

LXXIX.

Of that saying Alvar Fañez was glad when the Cid spake.
Don Jerome his ordination there and then they undertake.
In Valencia great riches have they given to his hand.
God! how merry was all Christendom that now within the land
Of Valencia a bishop of reverend grace had they!
Glad therefore was Minaya and took leave and went his way.

LXXX.

And now is all Valencia in peaceable estate.
Minaya Alvar Fañez to Castile departed straight;
His halts I will pass over, nor renew them to the mind.
But he sought out Alphonso where the King was to find.
The King to Sahagun had gone before some little space,
But was come back to Carrión; he might find him in that place.
Minaya Alvar Fañez was glad when this was known.
With his presents he departed forthwith to Carrión.

LXXXI.

Now whn the mass was over, thence did Alfonso rise,
And Minaya Alvar Fañez came there in noble guise..
In the presence of the people he kneeled upon his knee
He fell at don Alphonso's foot, and bitter tears shed he.
He kissed his hands; unto the King most lovely words he spake:

LXXII.

"A boon my lord Alfonso for the Creator's sake!
My lord Cid of the battles has kissed thy hands ere now,
Thy hands and thy feet likewise, for his noble lord art thou,
If thou favorest him, God's favor come upon thee from above.
Thou didst send him into exile and bearest him no love,
Though in strange lands he thriveth. Jérica he won in war

And Onda, so they call it; so also Almenár,
And likewise Murviédro (for a greater town 'tis known),
And he has ta'en Cebólla and further Castejón
And he has stormed Peñacadéll that is a place of power.
He is master of Valencia and these places at this hour.
With his own hand the great Campeador a bishop hath ordained.
He has forced five pitched battles and in each three victory gained.
The gift of the Creator was a very mighty prey,
Do thou behold the tokens of the truth of that I say:
Here be an hundred horses that in strength and speed excel;
With bridle and with saddle each one is furnished well.
He kissed thy hands and begged thee thine acceptance to accord.
He declares himself thy vassal, and owns thee for his lord."

The King has lifted his right hand and crossed himself thereon:
"With what a wondrous booty the Campeador has won
I am well pleased in spirit. Saint Isidore to speed!
I am glad the Campeador does now so many a fair deed.
I accept the gift of horses that the Cid to me has sent"

Though the King thereby was gladdened, was Ordoñez not content;

"Meseems that in the Moorish land is no man any more,
Since so his will upon them works the Cid Campeador."

To the Count the King gave answer: "So speak not of him now!
In faith he doth me service of a better sort than thou."

And then outspoke Minaya, like a nobleman spoke he:
"The Cid, if it shall please thee, desires a boon of thee,
For his wife Dame Xiména and his daughters two beside,
That they may leave the convent where he left them to abide,
And may hasten to Valencia to the noble Campeador."
Then said the King in answer: "My heart is glad therefor.
That they be given escort I will issue the command,
So that they may be protected as they travel through my land
From insult and dishonor and whatever harm may be.
And when these ladies shall have reached my kingdom's boundary,
Have a care how thou shalt serve them, thou and the Campeador.
Now hark to me, my vassals, and my courtiers furthermore:
I like not that to Roy Diaz any losses shall befall,
And therefore to his vassals, the Cid their lord that call,
I restore that which I seized on, their possession and their fee.
Let them keep their lands, no matter where the Campeador may be
From harm and hurt the safety of their persons I accord.

This I do that they may lightly render service to their lord."

Minaya Alvar Fañez kissed the King's hand straightway.
And the King smiled upon him and a fair word did he say:
"Who'er to serve the Campeador desireh now to ride,
As for me, he has permission, and God's grace with him abide.
More than by further hatred by this measure shall we gain."

Counsel straightway together held the Heirs of Carrión twain.
"The fame of the Cid Campeador grows great on every side,
An we might wed his daughters, would our needs be satisfied.
Scarce we dare frame this project e'en to ourselves alone;
The Cid is of Bivár, and we are Counts of Carrión."

They hatched that plot between them, to none they told the thing.
Minaya Alvar Fañez took leave of the good King:.
"Ha! goest thou, Minaya? The Creator give thee grace.
Take an herald. As I deem it he may help thee in this case.
If thou take the ladies, serve them even as they desire.
Even unto Medína grant them all that they require.
The Campeador shall take them in his charge thenceforward on."
After leave ta'en Minaya from the court he got him gone.

LXXXIII.

And so the Heirs of Carrión did each with each consent.
With Minaya Alvar Fañez in company they went:
"In all things thou excellest; likewise in this excel:
Greet now my lord Cid of Bivár for us exceeding well,
To the utmost of our effort his partisans are we.
The Cid, an he will love us, shall get no injury."
Said Minaya: "In that proffer naught displeasing I discern."

Gone is Minaya. Home again did the two counts return.
He hastens to San Pedro where the three ladies are.
Very great was the rejoicing when they saw him from afar.
To offer prayer Minaya to San Pedro did descend.
He turned back unto the ladies when the prayer was at an end.
"I greet thee, Dame Xiména. God thee prosper and maintain,
And so likewise thy daughters, the noble children twain.
In the city where he dwelleth the lord Cid greets thee fair.
Good health has he and riches that are beyond compare.
The King for a gift to him your freedom gave to me,
To take you to Valencia our land of lawful fee.
If the Cid might behold you well and unharmed again,

He would be all rejoicing, but scant would be his pain."
"May the Creator so decide," the Dame Xiména said.
Minaya Alvar Fañez sent three horsemen on ahead,
To the Cid within Valencia the men did he commend:
"Announce unto the Campeador, whom the Lord God defend,
That the King his wife and daughters has released unto my hands,
And has ordered escort for us as we travel through his lands.
Fifteen days from this time forwar, if God keep us in his care,
With his wife and with his daughters I will come unto him there,
With the noble ladies also their servitors that be."
The riders are gone forward, to the matter they will see.

Minaya Alvar Fañez in San Pedro did abide.
There might you see the household swarming in from every side;
Unto my lord Cid of Bivár in Valencia would they go.
They besought Alvar Fañez that he would them favor so.
To them replied Minaya. "That will I gladly do."
And five and sixty horsemen have swelled his retinue,
And he had brought an hundred thither in his command.
To accompany the ladies, they arrayed a noble band.

Minaya marks five hundred to the Abbot then gave o'er.
I will tell how he expended other five and twenty score.
Xiména the good lady and likewise her daughters twain,
And they that served before her, the women of her train,
To deck out all those ladies good Minaya did prepare
With the best array in Burgos, that he might discover there,
And the mules and palfreys likewise that they might be fair to see.
When he had decked the ladies in this manner beautifully,
Got ready good Minaya to ride upon his way.
Lo now! Raquél and Vidas. Down at his feet fell they:
"A boon! true knight, Minaya! If the Cid stand not our aid,
He has ruined us. If only the amount to us were paid
We would forego the usury!" "So will I tell the Cid,
If God bring me there. High favor shall there be for what ye did.
Answered Raquél and Vidas: "The Creator send it so.
If not, we will leave Burgos in search of him to go."

Minaya Alvar Fañez to San Pedro got him gone.
Many people came around him as he started to ride on.
At parting from the Abbot great grief of heart was there:
"Minaya Alvar Fañez, God keep thee in his care.
The hands of the good Campeador, I prithee kiss for me
That he may keep the convent still in his memory,
And always may endeavor to make it prosper more,

So shall increase the honor of the Cid Campeador."
"Right gladly will I do it," Minaya straight replied.
Their leave then have they taken and fettled them to ride,
And with them went the herald on their need that was to wait.
Through the King's realm an escort they gave them very great.
From San Pedro to Medína in five days time they passed.
Lo, the dames and Alvar Fañez to Medína came at last!

I will tell you of the horsemen that brought those tidings through.
When my lord the good Cid of Bivár thereof the import knew,
He was glad at heart and merry. His voice he lifted straight:
"Who sends a noble messenger, should like return await.
Munio Gustióz, Per Vermudóz, the first of all are you,
And Martin Antolínez from Burgos, tried and true,
And Jerome the bishop also, a worthy clerk is he,
With a hundred ride you ready to fight if need shall be.
Through Saint Mary's to Molína further onward shall ye wend;
Avelgalvon there holds sway my vassal and my friend.
With another hundred horsemen he will watch you on your way.
Ride forth unto Medína with all the speed ye may,
With Minaya Alvar Fañez my wife and daughters there
Haply ye shall discover as the messengers declare.
Bring them hither to me nobly. In Valencia I will bide,
That cost me dear. Unguarded 'twere madness undenied
To leave it. 'Tis my portion. There will I stay therefore."

They fettled them for riding, when all his words were o'er;
With utmost speed they hastened, their march they would not stay.
They have passed by Saint Mary 's. At Froncháles rested they.
Next day into Molína, their halting-place, they spurred.
When those tidings the Morisco Avengalvón had heard,
To welcome them with joyance unto them did he descend:
"Are you then come the vassals of my heart's dearest friend?
Be it known it grieves me little. Therein my joy is great."

And Muño Gustióz answered, for no man would he wait:
"My lord Cid sends thee greeting, as also his command
That with an hundred horsemen thou shalt serve him out of hand.
In the city of Medína lie his wife and danghters twain.
Thou wilt go for them straightway and bring them here again,
Even unto Valencia thou shalt not from them part."
Avengalvón gave answer: "I will do it with glad heart."
That night he chose them escort, a mighty band were they.
In the morning they got ready anew to take the way.
They asked for but an hundred; ten score had he forby.

They passed across the mountains that we re so steep and high,
And through the thicket of Toránz, so strong they had no dread.
And along through Arbujuélo adown the vale they sped.

Now round about Medína they watched on every side,
Minaya Alvar Fañez that armed train descried.
He was afraid and sent two knights the meaning to make plain.
They delayed not, to discover his desire their hearts were fain.
One stayed, to Alvar Fañez the other came once more:
"A company to seek us comes from the Campeador.
Per Vermudóz, lo, foremost among those ranks is he,
And likewise Muño Gustióz that frankly loveth thee,
And Martin Antolínez that was born in Burgos town,
And don Jerome the Bishop of honorable renown.
Avellgalvon the Castellan bringeth his host with these,
In eagerness the honor of my lord Cid to increase.
They march along together. They will be here anon."
Said Minaya: "Forth now let us ride." And swiftly was it done,
They would not stay. An hundred most splendidly arrayed
Sallied forth on noble horses with trappings of brocade.
Bells hung upon the martingales, the knights their bucklers bore
At the neck, and carried lances whence flew the flags of war
That Alvar Fañez' wisdom to all they might reveal,
And in what guise with those ladies he had issued from Castile.
All they that reconnoitering before the army ran
Now lifted up their weapons, and to make good cheer began.
Great mirth was there when all the rest to the Jalón drew nigh.
When they came unto Minaya they did him homage high.
And when Avengalvón was come, and might Minaya see,
Then forward to embrace him with smiling lips came he.
On the shoulder he saluted him, for such was still his way:
"O Minaya Alvar Fañez! For thee what glorious day!
Thou bringest here these ladies, whence we shall have great good,
The fighting Cid his consort, and the daughters of his blood.
We all shall do thee honor for his fortune groweth great.
Though we wished him ill, we cannot diminish his estate;
He will have alway our succor either in peace or war.
The man who will not know the truth, he is a dolt therefor."

LXXXIV.

Minaya Alvar Fañez, on his lips a smile broke out:
"Ha now! Ha now! Avengalvón. Thou art his friend no doubt.
If God shall bring me to the Cid and him alive I see,
The things that thou has done for us shall greatly profit thee.

Let us to our lodging, supper they have made ready there."
Avengalvón gave answer: "'Tis a courtesy most fair;
Double will I repay it ere the third morning fall."
To the town they came. Minaya provided for them all.
The escort that came with them, they were gladdened when they saw.
Minaya the King's herald commanded to withdraw.
The lord Cid in Valencia was greatly honored then,
When they gave such entertainment in Medína to his men.
The King paid for all. Minaya therefor had naught to pay.

At length the night was over, and came the break of day.
And mass they heard, and after away they rode at last.
They hastened from Medína, o'er the Jalón they pased.
And down the Arbujuélo, spurring apace they ride.
In haste the meadows of Toránz they cross from side to side,
They came unto Molína where Avengalvón was lord.
Bishop Jerome, a Christian worthy of his deed and word,
Escorted the three ladies whether by day or night,
And he led a good charger with his armor on his right.
And he and Alvar Fañez rode aye together thus.
They have entered in Molína the rich and glorious,
And loyally Avengalvón the Moor has served them there.
Unto the height of their desire, nothing they lacked whatever:
He even bade men strike for them the horseshoe from the steed.
Minaya and the ladies, God! he honored them indeed
They got them upon horseback when the next morning fell.
Unto Valencia loyally he served them all and well.

The Moor spent of his own estate, for naught from them took he.
With such honorable matters and mirth and revelry
They came nigh unto Valencia, that three leagues off doth stand.
To my lord Cid who in good hour had girded on the brand,
In the city of Valencia the news thereof they bore.

LXXXV.

Nothing had ever gladdened him so much as this or more,
For now there came good news of them for whom great love he had.
Straightway two hundred horsemen to go forth to them he bade,
To the good dames and Minaya fair reception to afford.
But he tarried in Valencia to watch it and to ward,
For he knew that Alvar Fañez with all due care would come.

LXXXVI.

And lo! now the two hundred welcomed Minaya home.
And the ladies and the daughters and all within the band.
The Cid to them within his train had issued his command
To ward full well the citadel, and the towers that were so high,
And the gates that none might enter and none depart thereby.
And he bade bring Baviéca that a little time before
From the King of Seville he had taken, when he routed him in war.
The Cid that in good season girt the brand on, of that steed
Knew not if he were swift to run or to stop short at need.
At the gateway of Valencia where none might work him woe,
Unto his wife and daughters he desired his gear to show.

When the ladies with great honor the host had welcomed home,
Then first into the city came the Bishop don Jerome.
He left his horse; to chapel straightway the Bishop wet.
With all men that he could gather who were of like intent
And surplice-clad, with crosses of silver, once again
They greeted good Minaya and the ladies of the train.
He who was born in happy time tarried but little there.
He has put on his surcoat. His beard was long and fair.
On Baviéca saddle and caparisons they threw.
The Cid took wooden weapons; forth on the steed he flew.
Leaped the steed Baviéca. With a great rush did he run.
'Twas rare to see. And when he ceased they marvelled all and one.
From that day Baviéca in all Spain had renown.
When that career was ended, from the steed the Cid got down,
And hastened forth his lady and daughters twain to greet.
When Dame Xiména saw him she cast her at his feet:
"Brand thou girdest in good season. Thy favour, Campeador!
Thou hast brought me forth from insults that were exceeding sore.
Look on me, lord! Look also on my daughters as on me.
By Glod's help and thine they are noble, and gently reared they be.

And the Cid straightway embraced them, mother and daughters twain.
Such joy they had that from their eyes the tears began to rain.
His men rejoiced. The quintains, they pierced them with the spear.
He who girt sword in a good time, hark what he said and hear.

"Oh thou my Dame Xiména, beloved and honored wife,
And ye two both my daughters that are my heart and life,
To the city of Valencia now do yet enter in,
The fair estate that for you it was my lot to win."

His hands they have kissed straightway, the daughters and their dame.
So with exceeding honor to Valencia they came.

LXXXVII.

With them the lord Cid hastened to the citadel apace,
He has ta 'en the ladies straightway up to the highest place.
And forth in all directions they turn their lovely eyes,
And they behold Valencia and how the city lies,
And in another quarter they might perceive the sea.
They look on fertile meadows close sown and great that be,
And on all things whatever that were of fair estate
God they praised with hands uplifted for that good prize and great.

My lord Cid and his followers thereof were glad and fain.
And now was winter over, for March would come again.
And of the countries oversea 'tis my desire to tell,
Even of the King Yússuf in Morocco that did dwell.

LXXVIII.

The King's heart of Morocco 'gainst the Cid was full of rage.
"By force the man hath entered into my heritage,
And giveth thanks to no one save Jesus Christ therefor."

And the King of Morocco gathered his hosts of war.
With fifty times a thousand under arms, good men and stark,
They put to sea. In galleons that army did embark
To seek the Cid Rodrigo in Valencia they went,
The ships came in; and straightway issued forth that armament.

LXXXIX.

To Valencia that the Cid had ta'en, 'twas thither they did fare.
The unbelievers haltccl and pitched pavilions there.
With tidings of the chances to my lord the Cid they came.

XC.

"Now thanks to the Creator and the Holy Father's name.
All the goods in my possession, I have them here with me.
Hardly I took Valencia, but I hold it for my fee;
This side death, I cannot yield it. Glory to God again
And to Holy Mary Mother that my wife and daughters twain
Are here with me. From oversea cometh now my delight.

Never will I forego it, I will take the arms of fight.
My lady and my daughters shall see me lift the brand,
They shall see how men build houses here in a foreign land,
And how a livelihood is won their eyes shall see it well."

He took his wife and daughters up to the citadel.
They raised their eyes and men they saw pitching tents everywhere.
"Cid, what is this? So may the Lord still keep thee in His care."
"Ha, wife, much honored! Therefor prithee be not troubled thus.
'Tis wealth most great and wondrous that they gather here for us.
Scarce art thou come, when presents they would give thee in that hour.
Thy daughters wait for marriage 'tis these that bring the dower."
"Unto thee, Cid, and unto God do I give thanks again"
"My lady in the palace in the citadel remain.
When thou seest me in battle, fear not at all for me.
By Saint Mary Mother's mercy, by God His charity,
That thou art here before me, my heart grows great within.
With God His help, this battle I certainly shall win."

XCI.

Now pitched are the pavilions. Apace the morning comes.
And furiously the heathen beat loud upon the drums.
"'Tis a great day," with a glad heart so now the lord Cid spake.
But his lady was sore frighted, her heart was like to break;
The ladies and his daughters were likewise all forlorn.
Never had they heard such a din since the day when they were born.

Therewith the great Cid Campeador with his hand he plucked his beard.
"This shall all be to your vantage. Therefore be not afeard.
Ere fifteen days are over, if so God's will it be,
We shall take those drums and show them you. What they are then shall
    you see.
And then unto the Bishop don Jerome they shall be given;
They will hang them in Saint Mary's, Mother of the Lord in Heaven."

It was a vow most solemn that my lord the Cid had made.
Now merry were the ladies and not so much afraid.
Those Moors out of Morocco in mighty haste they sped,
And on into the gardens they entered without dread.

XCII.

That thing beheld the outpost. He let the tocsin sound.
Of the Cid Roy Diaz ready were the companies around.

They sallied from the city with their arms appointed well.
When they came on the Moriscos upon them swift they fell.
They drove them from the gardens in exceeding sorry plight;
Of the Moors a full five hundred they slaughtered in that fight.

XCIII.

Even to the pavilions the pursuers would not slack;
They had done much and nobly when they thought of turning back.
There Alvar Salvadórez a prisoner did remain.
Then those that ate his bread returned to the lord Cid again.
With his own eyes he beheld it, to his face they spake thereon;
My lord the Cid was gladdened of the deeds that they had done.
"My knights we cannot other. Then harken unto me:
'Tis a noble day, yet nobler will tomorrow's battle be.
Arm you ere dawn. The Bishop don Jerome our souls will shrive,
Saying mass for us ere at them we are ready to let drive.
It shall be in no other fashion, we will go smite the foe,
In God's name and his Apostle's the good Saint James also.
For better fight than let them in the land devour our bread."
"With a good will and gladly," in reply to him they said

And then outspake Minaya, for nothing tarried he:
"Since thou wishest this, give orders of another sort to me.
For the sore need of battle grant me six score horse and ten;
From the far flank, when thou charges will I fall on them then.
On one side or the other the Lord will stand our stead."
"With right good will," unto him answered the Cid and said.

XCIV.

And now broke forth the morning, and now drew back the night.
Those bands of Christ delayed not to get ready for the fight.
At the middle cocks ere morning, mass for them Jerome did chant,
And mass said, absolution in full to them did grant:

"Who face to face shall perish this day the fight within,
May Christ receive his spirit, on my soul I take his sin.
Cid, don Rodrigo, in good hour thou girdedst brand; to thee
I sang the mass this morning. Grant then my boon to me:
Give me to strike the foremost the first stroke of the war."
"The thing to thee is granted," answered the Campeador.

XCV.

Out through the Quarter Towers full armed away they went.
The lord Cid and his henchmen did counsel and consent.
Levies they left behind them, the gates to watch and keep.
On the steed Baviéca sprang the lord Cid with a leap.
Fair trappings and caparisons girded that steed about.
With the standard from Valencia forthwith they sallied out.
Were with the Cid four thousand less but a score and ten,
They came gladly to a battle against fifty thousand men.
Alvar Alvarez and Minaya on the other side did smite.
It seemed good to the Creator, and they threw them into flight.
With the lance the Cid did battle, hand he set to sword as well.
So many Moors he slaughtered that their numbers none might tell.
Down from his elbow streaming the blood of battle came.
Even against King Yússuf three buffets did he aim.
He 'scaped from underneath the sword for his steed could run apace,
And bore him to Culléra, an exceeding mighty place.
Even so far he of Bivár pursued them as they fled,
With a host of gallant vassals in his company that sped.
He who in happy hour was born from that pursuit turned back;
He was gladdened of the booty they had taken inthe attack.
Good to him seemed Baviéca from head to tail that day.
In his hands remained the booty of that battle for a prey.
Of the twoscore and ten thousand, when they were counted o'er,
There 'scaped out of that battle but an hundred men and four.
My lord the Cid his henchmen have sacked the field around;
Of the gold and of the silver three thousand marks they found,
And of the other booty was no measure to be had.
My lord Cid and his vassals were all exceeding glad,
For in winning of the battle God's grace to them was shown,
When the king of Morocco in this guise was overthrown.
The Cid left Alvar Fañez to count the spoil and slain.
With fivescore horse he entered Valencia once again.
Helmless he rode. Upon his brow the coif was disarrayed.
Through the town on Baviéca he galloped, hand on blade.
And the ladies gave him welcome, on his coming that did wait.
My lord Cid stopped before them, reining in the charger great:
"Ladies, I bow before you. Groweth apace my fame.
While you have held Valencia in the field I overcame.
This was our God's desire and all his Saints likewise,
Since at your coming hither He gave us such a prize.
Look on the bloody sword-blade and the steed with sweat a-foam.
With such are the Moriscos in the battle overcome.
Pray now to God that I may yet live some few years from this;

You shall enter to great honor and men your hands shall kiss."

So he spake as he dismounted. When on the ground stood he
When the dames and his daughters and his wife of high degree
Saw him get off, they kneeled them down before the Campeador:
"Thy will be done, and mayst thou live through many a long year more."

The Cid unto the palace returning then they brought;
They rested them on benches most exquisitely wrought:
"Ha! Dame Xiména, wife of mine, didst thou beg this of me?
These dames thou hast brought hither so well that wait on thee,
In marriage to my vassals I am fain to give them o'er,
And unto every lady for her dower marks ten score.
Men shall know of their good service, in the kingdom of Castile.
With my maids' affairs hereafter at our leisure we shall deal."
All there rose up together, and kissed his fingers straight,
The rejoicing in the palace it was exceeding great.
As my lord Cid commanded so they brought the thing about.

Minaya Alvar Fañez tarried on the field without,
With his men to write and reckon. Arms, tents and rich array
In great store they discovered. It was a sovran prey.
The richest of the treasure I am fain now to recite:
The tale of all the horses they could not take aright;
They wandered all caparisoned. Was none to take a steed.
The Moors out of their provinces had gathered wealth indeed.
Though this were so, were given to the gallant Campeador
Of the best of all the horses for his share fifty score.
When the Cid had so many the rest content might bide.
What store of rich pavilions and carven poles beside
To the lord Cid and his vassals by the chance of war did fall,
And the King's tent of Morocco was the richest of them all,
All gold wrought are the tent-poles that pavilion that sustain.
My lord Cid the great Campeador did at that time ordain
That it stand pitched; to move it let not a Christian dare.
"Since hither from Morocco is come a tent so fair,
To Alfonso the Castilian I am fain to send it now;
That the Cid hath captured somewhat then lightly will be trow."

Laden with mighty riches to Valencia came they home.
That very noble cleric, the Bishop don Jerome,
When a surfeit of the fighting he had had of his hands twain,
Was at a loss to number the Moors that he had slain.
What fell to him of booty was sovran great of worth.
My lord Cid don Rodrigo (in a good time was his birth,)

Of all his fifth share of the spoil has sent him the tenth part.

XCVI.

The Christians in Valencia were all right glad of heart,
For now excelling riches, horses and arms they had.
Xiména and her daughters all three were passing glad,
And the other dames; as wedded upon themselves looked they.
And my lord Cid the noble in no wise would delay.
"Where art thou brave Minaya? Come hither to me now.
For thy great share of booty, no gratitude hast thou?
Of this my fifth of all the prey, I tell thee clear and plain,
Take unto thy good pleasure, but let the rest remain.
And tomorrow in the morning thou shalt certainly ride out
With the horses of my portion that I captured in the rout,
With the saddles and the bridles and the swords that them behove,
For the sake of my lady and for my daughters love.
Since Alfonso sent the ladies whither they were content,
These same two hundred horses to him thou shalt present,
That of him who rules Valencia the King no ill may say."

He bade go with Minaya Per Vermudóz straightway.
The next day in the morning they departed with all speed,
And a full two hundred henchmen along with them they lead,
With greetings from the Cid who fain would kiss his hands aright.
Even out of the battle where my lord Cid won the fight,
For a gift he sent Alfonso of horses good ten score:
"While I have breath within me, I will serve him evermore."

XCVII.

They have issued from Valencia. And they fettle them to fare.
They must watch well so mighty a booty do they bear.
And night and day they hastened for they gave themselves no rest.
The mountains that divide the lauds they have passed o'er the crest.
And the folk they fell to asking where Alfonso

XCVIII.

O'er the mountains, o'er the rivers, o'er the hills they took the road.
And at length before Valladolíd where the King lay they were.
Minaya and Per Vermudóz sent tidings to him there,
That reception to their followers he might bid his men extend.
"My lord Cid of Valencia presents with us doth send."

XCIX.

Glad was the King. Man gladder you never yet did see.
He commanded all his nobles to ride forth hastily.
And forth among the first of them did King Alfonso go,
Of him who in good hour was born the tidings for to know.
Know you the Heirs of Carrión happed in that place to be,
Also Count don García the Cid's worst enemy.
Of the tidings some were merry, and some were all folorn.
They caught sight of his henchmen who in happy hour was born.
They feared it was an army for no herald came before.
Straightway the King Alfonso crossed himself o'er and o'er.
Minaya and Per Vermudóz came forward with all speed,
They leaped from the saddle, they dismounted from the steed.
Before the King Alfonso upon their knees they fell.
They kissed the ground beneath him, the kissed his feet as well:
"Now a boon, King Alfonso. Thou art great and glorious.
For my lord Cid the Campeador do we embrace thee thus.
He holds himself thy vassal; he owns thee for his lord.
He prizes high the honor thou didst to him accord.
O King, but a few days agone in the fight he overcame
The King out of Morocco, Yússuf (that is his name),
With a host of fifty thousand from the field he drove away.
The booty that he captured was a great and sovran prey.
Great wealth unto his followers because of this did fall.
He sends thee twoscore horses and doth kiss thy hands withal.
Said King Alfonso:
"Gladly to accept them am I fain.
To the Cid who sent me such a gift I send my thanks again.
When I do unto his liking, may he live to see the day."

Thereat were many of good cheer and kissed his hands straightway.
Grieved was Count don García. Wroth was his heart within.
Apart he wells a little with ten men of his kin:
"A marvel is this matter of the Cid, so grows his fame.
Now by the honor that he hath we shall be put to shame.
Kings he o'erthroweth lightly, and lightly bringeth steeds
As though he dead had found them; we are minished by his deeds."

C.

Hear now of King Alfonso what he said upon this score:
"Thanks be to the Creator and the lord Saint Isidore
For the two hundred horses that the Cid to me hath sent.
Yet shall he serve me better in this my government.

To Minaya Alvar Fañez and Per Vermudóz I say
That you forthwith clothe your bodies in honorable array,
And as you shall require it of me take battle-gear
Such as before Roy Diaz in good manner shall appear.
Take then the gift I give you even these horses three.
As it seems to my avisement, as my heart telleth me,
Out of all these adventures some good will come to light."

CI.

They kissed his hands and entered to take their rest that night.
In all things that they needed he bade men serve them well.

Of the two Heirs of Carrión now am I fain to tell,
How secretly they counselled what thing should be their cast:
"Of my lord Cid the high affairs go forward wondrous fast.
Let us demand his daughters that with them we may wed.
Our fortune and our honor thereby may be well sped."
Unto the King Alfonso with their secret forth went they.

CII.

"As from our King and master a boon of thee we pray
By favor of thy counsel we desire to obtain
That thou ask for us in marriage of the Cid his daughters twain.
With honor and with profit shall the match for then, be fraught."

Thereon for a full hour's space pondered the King and thought
"I cast out the good Campeador, and wrong I do him still
For his good to me. I know not if the match be to his will,
But we in hand will take it, since so your pleasures tend."

Alvar Fañez and Per Vermudóz, for them the King let send.
He took them to a hall apart: "Now harken to me both
Minaya and Per Vermudóz. The Cid my service doth;
The Campeador, his pardon well hath he earned of me.
And shall have it. I will meet him, if so his will shall be.
In parley other tidings of my court I will make known;
Dídago and Ferrándo, the Heirs of Carrión,
Are fain to wed his daughters. Bear ye the message well,
And I pray you that these tidings to the Campeador ye tell.
It will be unto his honor, great will his fame have grown,
When he becomes the father of the Heirs of Carrión."

Minaya spake: (Per Vermudóz was glad of that he spake)

"To ask him thy desire we will even undertake.
And the Cid shall do thereafter as his pleasure shall decide."

"Say to the Cid Roy Diaz that was born in a glad tide,
That I will parley with him in the best place he may,
And there shall be the boundary wherever he shall say.
To my lord Cid in all things will I show my favor plain."

Unto the King they gave farewell, and got them gone again,
And onward to Valencia they hastened with their force.

When the good Campeador had heard, swiftly he got to horse,
And came to meet them smiling, and strong, embraced the two.
"Minaya and Per Vermudóz, ye are come back anew!
There are not many countries where two such gallants dwell.
From my lord King Alfonso what tidings are to tell?
Is he content? Did he vouchsafe to take the gift from me?"

Said Minaya, "In his soul and heart right well content is he,
And his good will he sendeth unto thee furthermore."
Said the Cid: "To the Creator now mighty thanks therefor."

The Leonese Alfonso his pleasure they made known
That the Cid should give his daughters to the Heirs of Carrión.
He deemed it would make him glorious and cause his fame to grow.
And in all truth and honor would advise him even so.

When my lord the Cid had heard it, the noble Campeador,
Then a long time much pondering he turned the tidings o'er,
"For this to Christ my master do I give thanks again.
I was sent forth to exile and my honor suffered stain.
That which is mine I conquered by mine endeavor high.
Unto God for the King's favor a thankful man am I,
And that for them of Carrión they ask my daughters two.
Minaya and Per Vermudóz, thereof what thinketh you?"

"Whate'er shall be your pleasure, that is it we shall say."
Said the Cid: "The Heirs of Carrión, of a great line are they,
And they are proud exceeding, and their favor fair at court.
Yet ill doth such a marriage with my desire coport.
But since it is his pleasure that is of more worth than we,
Let us talk thereof a little, but secret let us be.
May the Lord God in Heaven accord us as is best."

"Besides all this Alfonso this word to thee addressed:

He would come to parley with thee in what place thou art fain.
He desireth well to see thee and honor thee again.
Then what to do is fittest ye might be well agreed."

Said the Cid: "Now by this saying I am well pleased indeed."

"Where thou wilt hold this parley" said Minaya, "ponder well.
"In that the king desired it, no wondrous thing befell,"
That wherever we might find him we might seek him in his way,
As to our King and Master, our high devoir to pay.
Haply we may desire what good to him shall seem.
Nigh to the river Tagus that is a noble stream,
If so my lord desire it, we will hold the parley there."

He wrote the letters straightway and sealed them well and fair.
And then unto two horsemen he gave the letters o 'er.
Whatso the King desireth, that will the Campeador.

CIII.

Unto the King much honored, the letters they present.
When he had looked upon them, then was his heart content.
"To the Cid who in good time girt brand my greeting do I send,
And let us hold the parley when three weeks are at an end.
If I yet live, then doubtless I shall wait him in that place."
They tarried not, but hastened home to the Cid apace.

On both sides for the parley they got ready point device.
In Castile was ne'er such foison of mules without a price,
Nor so many fair-paced palfreys, nor strong steeds swift to guide,
Nor so many noble pennons on the stout lances tied,
And shields whereof the bosses did with gold and silver shine,
Robes, furs and Alexandrian cloth of satin woven fine.
And the King gave his order, to send much victual there,
To the waters of the Tagus where the parley they prepare.
The King leads many a good troop, and Carrión's Heirs are gay.
And here they run in debt apace, and there again they pay,
For they thought to have great profit and increase manifold,
And whatso they should desire, goods of silver and of gold.
And now hath King Alfonso got swiftly to his horse,
With counts and little nobles and vassals in great force.
As for the Heirs of Carrión great companies they bring.
From León and from Galicia came much people with the King;
Know well, the levies of Castile, they are a countless train.
And straight unto the parley they rode with slackened rein.

CIV.

In the city of Valencia, my lord Cid Campeador
Did not tarry, but the parley, he prepared himself therefor.
There were stout mules a-many and palfreys swift to course,
Great store of goodly armour, and many a fleet war-horse,
Many fair cloaks and mantles, and many skins withal;
In raiment of all colors are clad both great and small.
Minaya Alvar Fañez and Per Vermudóz that wight,
Martin Muñoz in Montemayór that held the rule of right,
And Martin Antolínez that in Burgos had his home,
And that most worthy cleric, the Bishop don Jerome,
And with Alvar Salvadórez Alvar Alvarez beside,
And likewise Muño Gustióz a gallant knight and tried,
Also Galínd Garcíaz, that in Aragon abode,
These to ride with the good Campeador got ready for the road.
And the people in the palace prepared them all and one.

Unto Alvar Salvadórez and the man of Aragon,
Galínd Garcíaz, his command has given the Campeador
That heart and soul Valencia they shall guard it and watch o'er.
And, moreover, all the others on their behests shall wait.
And my lord Cid has ordered that they bar the castle gate
And nowise throw it open either by night or day.
His wife and his two daughters within the hold are they,
Whom he loves best, and the ladies that do their pleasure still.
And he has so disposed it, even as a good lord will,
That not a soul among them shall venture from the tower,
Till to them he returneth, who was born in happy hour.

They issued from Valencia, forward they spurred along.
On their right were many horses, that were both swift and strong.
The Cid had ta 'en them. No man would have given him a steed.
And he rideth to the parley, the which he had decreed
With the King. In passage of a day, he came the King before.
When anear they saw him coming, the gallant Campeador,
With great worship to receive him, forth unto him they ride.
When he had looked upon them, who was born in a glad tide,
He halted his companions save his knights of dearest worth.
With fifteen of his henchmen he leaped down unto the earth,
As he who in good hour was born had willed that it should be.
Forthwith to earth he bends him on the hand and on the knee.
And the grass of the meadow with his very teeth he rent,
And wept exceeding sorely so great was his content.
How well unto Alfonso to do homage doth he know

And there before his sovereign's foot he cast him even so.
As for the King Alfonso, at heart it irked him sore:
"Rise up! Rise up upon thy feet, O thou Cid Campeador,
And kiss my hand, nor prithee in this guise my feet embrace,
And if thou wilt not do it, thou shalt not have my grace."
But natheless the good Campeador yet knelt on bended knee:
"As of my rightful master, I ask a boon of thee,
And namely that thy favor on me thou wilt bestow,
So that all men about us the thing may hear and know."

Said the King: "Now that right gladly and of good heart will I do;
And here I give thee pardon, and my favor I renew.
And thee unto my kingdom right welcome I will make."

My lord the Cid addressed him, after this wise he spake:
"Gramercy, lord Alfonso, I will take what thou hast given.
I will utter forth for this my thanks unto our God in Heaven,
And then to thee, and to the bands that round about me stand."

And on his knees yet kneeling, he kissed Alfonso's hand;
To his feet he rose, and on the lips greeted him with a kiss.
The others in the presence they were well pleased at this.
It irked Garci Ordoñez and Alvar Diaz sore.

My lord Cid spake and uttered this saying furthermore.

"To our Father and Creator I offer thanks again,
That my lord the King his pardon he vouchsafed me to attain.
In the day and the night season the Lord will cherish me.
Thou shalt he my guest, my master, if so thy pleasure be."
Said the King: "Today in no way were that seemly in my sight.
Thou art but now come hither, but we came in last night.
Today, therefore, Cid Campeador, thou shalt remain my guest,
And on the morrow morning we shall he at thy behest."

My lord the Cid has kissed his hand, granting it should be so.
Then came the Heirs of Carrión, their courtesy to show:
"We greet thee Cid. Thou wast brought forth in an hour of promise
   high.
And so far will we serve thee as in our power may lie."
"So grant it the Creator," to them the Cid replied.
The Cid my lord Roy Diaz, who was born in a good tide,
Unto the King his master was guest for that day's space,
Who could not let him from his sight, he held him in such grace.
At the Cid's beard grown so swiftly, long while the King did stare.

At the Cid much they marvelled, as many as were there.

And now the day was over, and upon them fell the night.
The next day in the morning the sun rose clear and bright.
The Cid had bidden his henchmen meat for all men to array.
With my lord Cid the Campeador so well content were they
That all were very merry, and moreover of one mind
That for three years together so well they had not dined.

The next day in the morning, when at last the sun outshone,
Then did Jerome the Bishop his matin song intone.
And when from mass they issued, all gathered in one place,
And the King did not tarry but began his speech apace:
"Hear me now, counts and nobles, and all my henchmen leal—
Unto my lord Cid Campeador I needst must make appeal.
God grant unto his profit that the thing may prove to be.
Dame Sol and Dame Elvíra, I ask their hands of thee,
That thou wilt in marriage give them to the Heirs of Carrión twain.
To me the match seems noble, and thereon there hangs much gain.
They ask them of thee. To that end I add my own command.
On my side and thine as many as round about us stand,
My henchmen and thy henchmen, let them therefor intercede.
Give them to us my lord the Cid. So God thee help and speed."
Said the Cid: "My girls to marry are hardly yet in state,
For their days are not many, nor are their ages great.
As for the Heirs of Carrión, much fame of them men say;
They suit well with my daughters, and for better e'en than they.
'Twas I begot my daughters, but thou didst rear the twain.
They and I for that bounty yet in thy debt remain.
Dame Sol and Dame Elvíra, unto thee do I present,
To whom thou wilt then give them and I will be content."

Said the King: "My thanks unto thee and to all the court I own."
Upon their feet got swiftly the Heirs of Carrión;
Of him who in good hour was born, lightly they kissed the hands.
Before the King Alfonso they made exchange of brands.

Out spake the King Alfonso like a man of gentle race:
"My thanks, so noble art thou, but first to God for grace
That for the Heirs of Carrión thou givest thy daughters twain.
Dame Sol and Dame Elvíra, in hand I have them ta'en.
To Carrión's Heirs as consorts those ladies I award.
I give away thy daughters as brides with thine accord,
May it please God that thou therewith in full content mayest rest.
Behold, the heirs of Carrión that wait on thy behest.

Let them go with thee, prithee, for I from hence must wend.
Three hundred marks of silver I give them to this end,
To spend upon the marriage or what else pleaseth thee,
Since within high Valencia in thy wardship they will be.
The sons and the daughters shall thy children be all four;
Whate'er shall be thy pleasure, do with them, Campeador."

The Cid received them from him, and the King's hand did kiss.
"My sovereign and my master, I think thee well for this.
Thou shalt give away my daughters, for I will not do the deed."
After the parle was over they gave pledges and agreed
That the next day in the morning when forth the sun should flame,
All persons at the parley should return to whence they came.
Thereby both fame and honor had the lord Cid Campeador,
And many mules and mighty, and fair palfreys furthermore,
And fine and precious raiment. And to give gifts he began,
Whatso he would to who would take, and denied it to no man.
As gifts full sixty horses did the lord Cid present.
Whoe'er was at the parley therewith was full content.
Now were they fain of parting, for night was like to fall.

The King the Heirs of Carrión took by the hand withal,
In the power of the Cid Campeador he put them both straightway.
"Behold them here thy children; since thy sons-in-law are they;
From this day forth do with them as thy heart shall give accord.
May they serve thee as their father, and keep thee for their lord."

"I thank thee and accept, O King, the gift which thou hast given.
Mayst thou be well rewarded by God who is in heaven.

CV.

"Of thee, my liege and sovran, a boon do I request
Since thou givest to wed my daughters in what way likes thee best,
Choose one my girls to give away, who in thy place shall stand,
Since thou hast them, I will never give them o'er with mine own hand.
To the Heirs. Such satisfaction to them shall be denied."
"Behold here Alvar Fañez," the King to him replied,
"Take them by the hand and give them to the heirs, even as I
Here afar off have ta ten them, as though I were hard by;
And throughout all the vigil their sponsor shalt thou be.
When again to me thou comest tell all the truth to me."

Said Alvar Fañez: "Faith! My lord, I am content indeed."

CVI.

To all this with due caution, know well they have agreed.
"Ha! King, my lord Alfonso much honored, for a sign
Of the parley that we held here, thou shalt take a gift of mine.
I bring thee thirty palfreys that are trapped rich and well,
And thirty fleet war-horses, each with a noble selle.
Take them and I will kiss thy hand."
The King Alfonso spake:
"Deep in thy debt thou hast me. Thy present I will take
Which thou givest. The Creator and all his saints accord
For the kindness thou hast done me that thou have a fair reward.
Oh my lord Cid Roy Diaz, thou hast done me honor high.
Full well thou cost my service, and well content am I.
Mayst thou reap of me some harvest ere my life be at an end.
Into God's hands I give thee. From the parley will I wend.
Hail God in Heaven! grant us our treaty well to keep."

CVII.

The Cid mounted Baviéca his charger at a leap.
"Here before my King Alfonso I say it openly,
Who would fain go to the marriage or would have a gift of me,
Let him come with me. His profit shall be great, as I conceive."

Now of his lord Alfonso the lord Cid took his leave..
His company he wished not, he departed from him straight.
There might you see a many of knights of fair estate
Taking leave of King Alfonso, that the while his hands did kiss:
"Let it be now thy pleasure, and prithee grant us this—
'Neath the Cid to great Valencia now will we march away
To see the Heirs of Carrión upon their wedding day,
And Dame Sol and Dame Elvíra that the Cid's daughters be."

Therewith the King was satisfied and gave them liberty.
And the King's bands diminished and the Cid's increased the more.
Great company of people marched with the Campeador.

They rode straight to Valencia ta'en when his star was high.
On Diégo and Ferrándo he bade them keep an eye.
Muño Gustióz and Per Vermudóz they had commandment plain—
In all my lord Cid's household were not a better twain
The ways of them of Carrión to discover them and find.
Ansuór Gonzálvez joined the Heirs who was a noisy hind,
Loose-tongued, and for untrustful in other things well known.

They showered many honors on the Heirs of Carrión.

Behold them in Valencia that the Cid my lord had ta'en.
When they looked upon the city they were exceeding fain.
Muño Gustióz and don Pero, to them the lord Cid spake:
"Straightway the Heirs of Carrión unto a lodging take,
But do you tarry with them, so doth my order run.
When entereth in the morning, when breaketh forth the sun,
Of Dame Sol and Dame Elvíra, their brides, they shall have sight."

CVIII.

Then every man departed to his lodging-place that night.
The Cid Campeador has entered his castle once again.
Abode him Dame Xiména, she and her daughters twain.

"Campeador who in good season girt sword, thou hast come thy ways;
May the eyes of our faces behold thee many days."

"I am come, wife much honored, by the Creator's grace,
And sons-in-law I bring thee, whence our fame shall wax apace.
I have married you well, my daughters, so thank me for it well.

CIX.

Forthwith a-kissing of his hands his wife and daughters fell,
And likewise all the ladies their pleasure still that did.
"Thanks be to the Creator and to thee, fair-bearded Cid,
What thing thou cost soever, it is well done indeed.
In all thy days thy daughters shall never be in need."

"When thou givest us in marriage, great wealth to us shall fall."

CX.

"Wife o'mine, Dame Xiména. praise God who made us all.
Dame Sol and Dame Elvíra, my girls to you I say,
From your marriage in all honor shall we increase alway.
But that I did not begin it, the truth now understand;
My lord Alfonso sought you and stately made demand
With such firm will, I wist not how to deny the thing.
And I put you both, my daughters, in the keeping of the King.
Know that he giveth you to wed, and that I am not the man."

CXI.

To make beautiful the palace, then one and all began.
There was displayed much arras on wall and pavement both,
Much purple and much samite and store of precious cloth.
'Twould have pleased you in that palace to have sat you down to eat.
And speedily together did his knights assembled meet.

And for the Heirs of Carrión as at that time they sent,
To horse they got and onward to the palace forth they went.
And fine is all their raiment, and stuff of proof likewise.
They came afoot and properly, God! in what lowly guise!
The Cid and all his vassals received them when they came.
They bowed the head before him; they bowed before his dame;
Straightway to take their places on a noble seat they strode.
Of my lord Cid all the henchmen exceeding wisdom showed,
His speech who in good hour was born in quiet they expect.

And now the noble Campeador hath risen up erect:
"Since such a deed is toward, why do we tarry here?
Come hither Alvar Fañez whom I cherish and hold dear.
My daughters twain, behold them, to thy hand I give them o'er.
Be it known so to perform it unto the King I swore,
To fail in our agreement is in no way mine intent.
To the Heirs of Carrión their brides, now with thine hand present;
Let them have benediction and speed the wedding through."

To him replied Minaya: "This will I gladly do."

The ladies rose. He gave them into Minaya's care.
To Carrión's Heirs, Minaya now doth his charge declare:
"Lo! Minaya here before you, ye brothers born that be!
By the hand of King Alfonso, who has laid this charge on me,
I give to you these ladies that are both of noble blood,
That to wife ye take them nobly and in fair guise and good."

And with a will and gladly to take their brides they came,
And they kissed the hands straightway of my lord Cid and his dame.

They came forth from the palace when all these things were done.
And then unto Saint Mary's in haste they got them gone.
Bishop Jerome his vestments swiftly to him has ta 'en,
And he abode the coming at the portal of the fane.
He has given them his blessing, and chanted mass in course.

When from the church they issued with speed they got to horse.
They hastened from Valencia forth on the sandy shore.
God! the Cid and his companions, how well their arms they bore!
He who in happy hour was born, three times hath changed his steed.
With what he saw my lord the Cid was well content indeed,
For the two heirs of Carrión have well their steeds bestrode.
With the ladies to Valencia then home again they rode.
In that fair hold resplendent was the wedding that they had.
To rear up seven quintains the Cid next morning bade;
Before they went to dinner, were the seven burst in twain.

Full fifteen days together at the wedding they remain.
The fifteen days well nigh are done; homeward the nobles ride.
My lord Cid don Rodrigo who was born in a good tide
Of the mules and the palfreys and the battle-chargers swift,
Of beasts alone an hundred has granted forth in gift,
And cloaks, fur capes, and raiment of other sort great store,
and bestowed wealth in money in abundance furthermore.
The vassals of my lord the Cid, for they had counselled so,
For their part bridal tokens upon the guests bestow.
He came by great possession whoso thereof was fain,
Who was at the bridal, wealthy came to Castile again.
Now are all these guests together about to ride away;
To Roy Diaz in good hour born their last devoirs they pay,
And likewise to the ladies, and his men of high descent.
My lord Cid and his vassals they left in high content.
They said much honor of them as was indeed their due.
Diégo and Ferrándo were passing merry too;
Of the Count don Gonzálvo they were the children twain.

And now the guests came homeward unto Castile again.
The Cid and his two sons-in-law in Valencia they stay.
There dwell the Heirs until two years have well nigh passed away.
It was a mighty welcome in that city that they had.
The Cid and all his vassals were all exceeding glad.
Saint Mary and our Father, may it please them to consent
That the Cid and he who wrought it with the bridal be content.
Of this Cantar the couplets come now unto their end.
The Saints and the Creator preserve you and defend.

CANTAR III

THE AFFRONT OF CORPES

CXII.

The Cid lay in Valencia with all his men beside;
With him the Heirs of Carrión his sons-in-law abide.
Upon his couch to slumber lay the good Campeador.
There fell a hard occasion, a thing they looked not for.
From his cage came forth the lion, from his bonds he broke away.
All men throughout the palace in mighty dread were they.
'Neath the arm the Campeador his men their mantles up have ta'en,
About his couch they gathered, and beside their lord remain.
As for Ferránd Gonzálvez the Heir of Carrión,
He saw no place to hide in; chamber or tower was none.
Beneath the seat he crouched him so mighty was his dread.
And Dídago Gonzálvez out through the doorway fled,
Crying aloud: "Wo! Carrión no more shall I behold."
Beneath a wine-press timber he hid in fear untold.
Thence he brought cloak and tunic all filthy and forlorn.

With that he woke from slumber, who in happy hour was born,
And saw his good men round his couch in a close ring that stood.

"Now what is this my henchmen ~ What is it that ye would?"

"Ha, worthy lord! The lion gave us a fearful fright."
The Cid leaned on his elbow, on his feet he leaped upright.
He flung his cloak on shoulder. Straight for the beast he made.
The lion when he saw him, so sorely was afraid
That before the Cid, low cowering, to earth his head he bent.
Hy lord Cid don Rodrigo him by the neck has hent.
He drew him and he dragged him and within his cage shut fast.
As many as heheld it thought it a marvel vast.

And then through the palace they returned unto the hall,
Of his sons the Cid made question, but found them not at all.
Though they shouted for them loudly, none answered to the hail.
And when at last they found them, oh, but their cheeks were pale!
Such mirth as in the palace was ye never saw before;
But to plague them was forbidden by the lord Cid Campeador.
Many thought that but for cowards themselves the twain had shown.
Sore grieved at what befell them were the Heirs of Carrión.

CXIII.

While thus the affair standeth wherein they had such shame,
A host out of Morocco to besiege Valencia came.
Their camp within the Quarter Field have they arrayed aright.
For fifty thousand chieftains pavilions have they pight.
'Twas the King Búcar if perchance of him ye e'er heard tell.

CXIV.

The Cid and all his henchmen, it pleased them passing well,
For so by the lord's favor their gain should grow the more.
But know the Heirs of Carrión at heart were very sore,
For they sáw of the Moriscos many and many a tent,
Which liked them not. The brothers forthwith apart they went.
"We would keep in mind our profit, nor for the loss have care.
And now within this battle we must needs do our share."
"Such a thing well may keep us from seeing Carrión more.
Widows will be the daughters of the good Campeador."

But Muñoz Gustióz heakened how in secret they conferred.
To the Cid Campeador he came with the tale of what he heard:
"The two Heirs thy sons-in-law, their courage is so strong,
Because they go to battle, for Carrión they long.
As God cherishes and keeps them, go bid them have good heart,
That they in peace may tarry, nor in battle have a part.
But with that we shall conquer, and God shall be our stay."

My lord Cid don Rodrigo with a smile went his way.
"My sons, the Heirs of Carrión. God have you in his care.
In your arms rest my daughters that as the sun are fair.
And as I yearn for battle, so of Carrión are ye fain.
In pleasance in Valencia to your hearts desire remain!,
For as for the Moriscos, them well enough I know,
And by grace of the Creator have courage to o'erthrow."

While they spoke thus, King Búcar sent word and commanded The Cid to quit Valencia and go his way in peace.*

Otherwise Búcar would exact payment for all that the Cid had done in the city. The Cid said to him who bore the message:

---

[4] At this point a lacuna occurs in the text of the poem. The prose passage is supplied from the Chronicle of the Twenty Kings, an emendation due to Pidal.

"Go thou and say to Búcar, that son of an enemy, that before three days are past, I will give him all that he asks."

The next day the Cid ordered all his men to take up their weapons, and marched out against the Moors. The Heirs of Carrión on that occasion sought the van of him. After the Cid had marshalled his men in order of battle, don Ferrándo, one of the Heirs, went forth to attack a Moor who was called Aladraf. The Moor, when he beheld don Ferrándo, came forward likewise to attack him. Thereupon the Heir of Carrión, being overcome with fear of the Moor, wheeled his horse and fled before him. Single-handed he dared not await the Moor's coming.

When Pero Vermudóz, who was hard by, beheld this, he attacked the Moor, fought with him and slew him. Then he took the Moor's horse and went in quest of the Heir who was in full flight.

"Don Ferrándo," he said to him, "take this horse and tell all men that thou didst slay the Moor, his master. I will be thy witness." And the Heir replied: "Don Pero Vermudóz, I thank thee greatly for what thou sayest.

"May I see that time when payment I shall make to thee twice o'er
For all that thou deserves". The twain turned back once more.
Don Pero there bore witness to Ferrándo's brag and lie.
The Cid and all his vassals were gladdened much thereby.

"If God our Father wills it, in Heaven that doth dwell,
My sons-in-law in battle shall both acquit them well."

So they spake. And the two armies now the advance began.
In the Moorish host resounded of the drums the rataplan.
It was among the Christians a marvel sore to some,
For never had they heard it, since but newly were they come.
On Diégo and Ferrándo greater wonder yet did fall,
And of their free will thither they would not have come at all.
To what he said who was brought forth in happy hour give ear:
"Ho! now don Pero Vermudóz, who art my nephew dear,
Dídago and Ferrándo now keep them well for me,
For in mine eyes my sons-in-law are dear exceedingly.
By God's help the Moriscos shall hold the field no more."

CXVI.

"In the name of every charity I tell thee, Campeador,
That today to be their keeper I never will remain.
To me they matter little—let him keep them who is fain.
I with my men about me against their van will smite;

Do thou with thine hold firmly the rearward of the fight.
Then canst thou aid me lightly if peril should arise."

Minaya Alvar Fañez came then to him likewise.
"Oh, Cid, give ear, and hearken, Oh faithful Campeador!
For surely in this battle shall God himself make war,
And He will make thee worthy with Him therein to share.
Where 'er thou deemest fitting bid us attack them there.
Each man must do his duty. Upon them let us thrust.
On God and on thy fortune now hangeth all our trust."
My lord Cid said: "Then prithee tarry here yet awhile."
Lo! don Jerome the Bishop who was armed in gallant style,
He stopped before the Campeador. Fair fortune had he aye.
"The Mass of Holy Trinity I sang for thee this day.
For this cause from mine own country did I seek thee and ensue,
Since in the slaughter of the Moor such great delight I knew.
And I am fain to honor both mine order and mine hand.
In the forefront of the battle it is my desire to stand.
And crosses on my pennant, and blazoned arms have I.
If it be God his pleasure, I am fain mine arms to try,
That so at last my spirit in perfect peace may be,
And thou mayst be, my lord the Cid, better content with me.
If thou cost me not this honor, from thy side I will retire."

The lord Cid gave him answer: "I am pleased with thy desire.
Of the Moors go make a trial, lo, where they are in sight.
From hence we shall behold it, how the Abbot fights the fight."

CXVII.

And don Jerome the Bishop went spurring thence away.
'Gainst the cnd of the encampment lie guided forth the fray.
By his good hap and God's mercy who ever loved him well,
At the first stroke he delivered two Moors before him fell.
When in twain his lance was broken, he set hand upon the blade.
Well was he tried. And Name of God! what a fair fight he made!
Two with the lance, and with the sword five of the foe he slew.
The Moors are very many. Around him close they drew,
They did not pierce his armour, though they laid on strokes of power.

His eyes beheld the Bishop, who was born in happy hour,
He caught his shield, the battle-spear he laid it low along,
He spurred Baviéca the well-paced steed and strong,
He went to smite against them with all his soul and heart.
The foremost ranks of battle did the lord Cid dispart:

Of the Moors he struck down seven, and five of them hath slain.
God was well pleased, the battle it was granted him to gain.
My lord Cid and his henchmen in hot pursuit they went.
There had you seen the stakes uptorn and may a tent-rope rent,
And all the ten-poles falling that were wrought so rich and brave.
From the tents, my lord Cid's vassals King Búcar's henchmen drave.

CXVIII.

Out of the tents they drave them; on them in pursuit they flew.
Many arms and many a hauberk, had you seen there cloven through,
And many a head well helmed in the battle fallen low,
And many a steed masterless that galloped to and fro.
For seven miles together they followed up the flight.
As he followed, on King Búcar the Cid my lord did light:
"Turn hither, Búcar. thou hast come from the land over sea.
The Cid whose beard is mighty thou shalt meet with presently.
Let us greet, and in fast friendship let each to each be bound."
To the Cid answered Búcar: "Such a friendship God confound.
A sword in hand thou bearest, and I see thee spur amain,
Seemeth well that thou upon me to try that blade art fain.
If my horse keep from stumbling and falleth not with me.
Thou shalt not overtake me till we ride into the sea."
My lord Cid answered: "With the truth that word no faith shall keep."
A good steed had Búcar that sprang off great leap on leap.
But the Cid's Baviéca upon him fast did gain.
Three fathoms from the water was Búcar overta 'en.
He has lifted up Coláda. A great stroke did he smite.
The carbuncles upon his heml he has smitten through forthright.
He cut straight through the helmet, all else in twain he crave,
And slashing to the girdle of the King came down the glaive.
Búcar the King from oversea the Cid hath overthrown.
Well worth a thousand golden marks was the great sword Tizón,
That he took there. 'Twas a victory most marvelous and great.
Here my lord Cid got honor and all that on him wait.

CXIX.

And now with all that booty, homeward again they wheeled.
And be it known that steadfastly they plundered all the field.
With him who in good hour was born to the fonts they came once
    more;
My lord the Cid Roy Diaz, the famous Campeador,
With two swords he greatly cherished through the carnage swiftly
    passed.

O'er his brow his cap was wrinkled, back was his mail-hood cast,
And but a little ruffled was the cap upon his hair.
On every side his henchmen came thronging to him there.
My lord the Cid saw somewhat and was well pleased thereby,
For he looked forth before him lifting up his eyes on high.
And Diégo and Ferrándo he beheld, that near him drew.
Of the Count don Gonzalvo the children were the two.
My lord the Cid smiled beautifully, for a glad man was he.

"Are ye come here, my sons-in-law? Ye are both sons to me.
I know that with the fighting ye are right well content.
To Carrión fair tidings that concern you shall be sent,
How by us the King Búcar unto defeat was thrust.
As sure as unto the Lord God and all his saints I trust,
With the rout of the foeman shall we all we be satisfied.
Minaya Alvar Fañez came now unto his side.
Hacked with the swords was all the shield that at his neck he wore.
The strokes of many lances had scarred it furthermore.
They that those strokes had stricken, had reaped therefrom no gain.
Down the blood streamed from his elbows. More than twenty had he
    slain.
"To God and to the Father on High now praises be,
And Cid who in good hour wast born so likewise unto thee.
Thou slewest the King Búcar, and we ha' won the day.
To thee and to thy vassals belongeth all the prey.
And as for thy two sons-in-law they have been proved aright,
Who got their fill of Moorish war upon the field of fight."

Said my lord Cid in answer, I therefore am right glad.
Since they are proved, hereafter in esteem shall they be had."

In honesty he said it, but a jest the thing they thought.
The prey unto Valencia they gathered and they brough't.
My lord the Cid was merry and his vassals with him there.
Six hundred marks of silver were allotted to his share.

The sons-in-law of my lord Cid, when they had ta'en away
Their war-prize, when the booty safe in their hand had they,
Took care that no decrease thereof should in their time be made.
In the city of Valencia they were splendidly arrayed,
Feeding well, and wearing noble cloaks and gallant capes of fur.
The Cid and all his henchmen exceeding glad they were.

CXX.

'Twas a great day in the palace of the Cid Campeador,
When he had slain King Búcar and they won the field of war.
He raised his hand, he plucked his beard: "To Christ now glory be,
Who is the Lord of all the Earth, for my desire I see,
That with me in the battle my two sons should front the foe.
Of them most noble tidings to Carrión shall go:
How they are greatly honored, and what renown they gain."

CXXI.

It was a mighty booty that the Cid his host had ta 'en.
Part is their own. In safety they kept the rest aside.
My lord the Cid gave orders who was born in a good tide,
That to all men of that conquest his true share they should allot,
And that the fifth of my lord Cid should nowise be forgot.
And all men did according, being prudent one and all.
For his fifth, six hundred horses to my lord Cid did fall,
And there were many camels and, moreover, mules as well.
Of them there were so many, that their number none might tell.

CXXII.

All of this prey was captured by the great Campeador:
"Now unto God be glory who is Lord the whole world o'er.
Before I was in poverty who have grown rich and great,
For now I have possessions, gold, honor, and estate;
And the two Heirs of Carrión my sons-in-law are they.
And since it is God's pleasure I win in every fray;
And the Moors and the Christians they have great dread of me.
And over in Morocco, where many mosques there be,
Where all men are in terror lest upon them I descend
On some fine night. That venture in no way I intend—
I shall not go to seek them. In Valencia I shall stay.
By God's aid, to me their tribute they shall render up and pay.
To me or unto whom I will, they shall pay the money down."

Very great was the rejoicing in Valencia the town
That rose in all the levies of the Cid Campeador,
That God's will hath vouchsafed them to triumph in the war.
Likewise of both his sons-in-law excelling was the mirth,
For each of them won booty five thousand marks in worth.
Themselves they deem right wealthy, those Heirs of Carrión twain.

And they with all the others to the palace came again.
With my lord the Cid the Bishop don Jerome standeth here.
And the good Alvar Fañez, the fighting cavalier.
Of the Campeador his household are many others by.
When the heirs of Carrión entered, they were given greeting high.
By Minaya for the sake of my lord Cid Campeador:
"Come, brothers, by your presence now are we honored more."
When they were come the Campeador was merry of his cheer:
"Lo! now behold, my sons-in-law, my faithful wife and dear,
With Dame Sol and Dame Elvíra that are my daughters twain,
Now nobly may they serve you and nobly entertain.
Now glory to Saint Mary, Mother of our Lord! God's name!
You are like from these your marriages to win abundant fame.
Unto the land of Carrión fair tidings shall be sped."

CXXIII.

Out spake the Heir Ferrándo when all the word was said:
"Glory to the Creator, and, noble Cid, to thee.
We have so many riches that numberless they be.
Through you we have much honor, and we have fought for you;
We conquered the Moriscos in the battle, and we slew
King Búcar, proven traitor, so pray you have a care
Now for some other matter; well marcheth our affair."

My lord the Cid his henchmen spake smiling round about
Of whoso fought most fiercely or best pursued the rout.

But Diégo and Ferrándo mid such men they did not find.
And now in all the japing the henchmen had designed
Both day and night together they mocked sore the Heirs again.
A very evil counsel together took the twain.
Verily they are brothers, forthwith apart they turn
To the thing that they have spoken, let us have no concern.
"Let us return to Carrión. Here overlong we wait.
The riches we have gathered are excellent and great.
We cannot hope to spend them in the mountance of our lives.

CXXIV.

"Now of the Cid the Campeador let us demand our wives.
Let us say that we will bear them to the lands of Carrión.
The place where they are heiresses shall unto them be shown.
We shall take them from Valencia, from the Campeador his reach.
And then upon the journey we shall work our will on each,

Ere the matter of the lion for a sore reproach and scorn
They turn to our discomfort who are heirs of Carrión born.
We shall bear with us of treasure nigh priceless a fair stock.
Of the daughters of the Campeador we two shall make our mock.
We shall be rich men always who possess such valiant things,
And fit to marry daughters of emperors or kings,
Who art the Counts of Carrión by virtue of our birth.
The Campeador his daughters we shall mock at in our mirth.
Ere the matter of the lion they throw at us in disdain."

When this they had decided the two returned again.
Ontspake Ferránd Golzalvez for silence in the Court:

"Cid Campeador, so may our God abide thy strong support,
May it please Dame Xiména, but first seem good to thee,
And Minaya Alvar Fañez and all men here that be
Give us our wives. By marriage are they ours in very deed.
Unto our lands in Carrión those ladies we will lead.
With the dower-lands to enfeoff them that we gave for bridal right
Of the lands of our possession, thy daughters shall have sight,
And those wherein the children to be born to us shall share."

The Cid my lord the Campeador scented no insult there:
"I shall give you my daughters and of my wealth dispone.
Ye gave them glebe of dowry in the lands of Carrión,
Three thousands marks of dower shall to my girls belong.
I will give mules and palfreys both excellent and strong,
And great steeds of battle swift and of mighty thew,
And cloth and silken garments with the gold woven through.
Coláda and Tizón the swords I will give to you likewise
Full well ye know I got them in very gallant guise.
My sons ye are, for to you do I give my daughters two.
My very heart's blood thither ye carry home with you.
In León and in Galicia and Castile let all men hear
How I sent forth my sons-in-law with such abundant gear.
And serve you well my daughters, your wedded wives that be.
An you serve them well rich guerdon ye shall obtain of me."
To this the heirs of Carrión their full assent made plain.
The daughters of the Campeador were given them and ta'en,
And they began receiving as the Cid's orders went.
When of all their heart's desire they were at last content,
Then Carrión's heirs commanded that the packs be loaded straight,

Through Valencia the city was the press of business great,
And all have taken weapons and all men gallop strong,

For they must forth the daughters of the Cid to speed along
Unto the lands of Carrión. To mount all men prepare,
Farewell all men are saying. But the two sisters there,
Dame Sol and Dame Elvíra, kneeled to the Cid Campeador:
"A boon, so may God keep thee, O father, we implore.

Thou begottest us. Our mother she brought us forth in pain.
Our liege-lord and our lady, here do ye stand ye twain.
Now to the lands of Carrión to send us is your will;
It is our bounden duty thy commandment to fulfil.
And so we two together ask but this boon of thee,
That in the lands of Carrión thy tidings still may be."
My lord the Cid has clasped them, and he has kissed the twain.

CXXV.

This hath he done. Their mother hath doubled it again.
"Go, daughters! the Creator of you henceforth have care
Mine and your father's blessing you still with you shall bear.
Go forth where you are dowered in Carrión to dwell.
I have, after my thinking, married you passing well."
The hands of their father and their mother kissed the two.
Blessing and benediction they gave to them anew.

My lord Cid and the others have fettled them to ride,
With armor and with horses and caparisons of pride.
From Valencia the splendid were the Heirs departing then.
They took leave of the ladies and all their bands of men.
Through the meadow of Valencia forth under arms they went.
The Cid and all his armies were very well content.
He who in good hour belted brand in signs had seen it plain
That these marriages in no way should stand without a stain.
But since the twain are married, he may not repent him now.

CXXVI.

"My nephew Felez Múñoz, I prithee where art thou?
Thou art my daughters' cousin in thy soul and in thine heart.
With them even unto Carrión I command thee to depart.
Thou shalt see what lands for dower to my girls are given o'er,
And shalt come again with tidings unto the Campeador."

Quoth Felez Múñoz: "Heart and soul that duty pleases me."
Minaya Alvar Fañez before the Cid came he:
"Back to the town of Valencia, Oh Cid, now let us go;

For if our God and Father the Creator's will be so,
To Carrión's lands thy daughters to visit we shall wend.
Dame Sol and Dame Elvíra, to God do we commend.
Such things may you accomplish as will make us glad and fain."

The sons-in-law gave answer: "Now that may God ordain."

They lamented much at parting. Daughters and sire wept sore,
So also wept the cavaliers of the Cid Campeador.
"Thou, cousin, Felez Múñoz, now hark to this aright.
Thou shalt go by Molína, and there shalt lie one night,
And greet fair the Morisco Avengalvón my friend;
That he may most fair reception to my sons-in-law extend.
Tell him I send my daughters to the lands of Carrión,
In all their needs his courtesy as beseemeth shall be shown.
Let him ward them to Medína for the love he beareth me.
For all that he cloth for them I will give him a rich fee."

They parted then, as when the nail out of the flesh is torn.

He turned back to Valencia who in happy hour was born.
And now the Heirs of Carrión have fettled them to fare.
Saint Mary of Alvarrazín, their halting-place was there.

From thence the Heirs of Carrión plied furiously the spur.
Ho! in Molína with the Moor Avengalvón they were.
The Morisco when he heard it in his heart was well content,
And forth with great rejoicings to welcome them he went.
Ah, God! how well he served them in what e 'er their joy might be!
The next day in the morning to horse with them got he.
He bade two hundred horsemen for escort forth to ride.
They crossed the mountains of Luzón (so are they signified),
And the Vale of Arbujuélo to the Jalón they came.
The place where they found lodging, Ansaréra is its name.
Unto the daughters of the Cid, the Moor fair presents gave,
And to either Heir of Carrión beside a charger brave.
For the love he bore the Campeador, all this for them he wrought.

They looked upon the riches that the Moor with him had brought
And then together treason did the brothers twain concert.
"Since the daughters of the Campeador we shortly shall desert,
If but we might do unto death Aengalvon the Moor,
The treasure he possesses for ourselves we should secure
Safe as our wealth in Carrión those goods we will maintain.
And ne'er will the Cid Campeador avenge on us the stain."

While they of Carrión this shame complotted each with each,
In the midst a Moor o'erheard them, that could of Latin speech.
He kept no secret. With it to Avengalvón he ran:
"Thou art my lord. Be wary of these persons, Castellan.
I heard the heirs of Carrión that plotted death for thee."

CXXVII.

This same Avengalvón the Moor, a gallant man was he
He got straightway on horseback with servitors ten score.
He brandished high his weapons, he came the Heirs before.
And the two Heirs with what he said but little pleased they are:
"If for his sake I forebore not, my lord Cid of Bivár,
I would do such deeds upon you as through all the world should ring,

And then to the true Campeador his daughters would I bring.
And unto Carrión never should you enter from that day.

CXXVIII.

What I have done against you, ho! Heirs of Carrión, say,
For without guile I served you, and lo, my death ye plot.
For wicked men and traitors I will leave you on the spot.
Dame Sol and Dame Elvíra with your good leave I go;
For of these men of Carrión I rate the fame but low.
God will it and command it, who is Lord of all the Earth.
That the Campeador hereafter of this match have joy and mirth."
That thing the Moor has told them, and back he turned him there.
When he crossed over thee Jalón, weapon he waved in air.
He returned unto Molína like a man of prudent heart.

And now from Ansaréra did Carrión's Heirs depart;
And they began thereafter to travel day and night.
And they let Atiénza on the left, a craggy height.
The forest of Miédes, now have they overpassed,
And on through Montes Claros they pricked forward spurring fast.
And then passed Griza on the left that Alamos did found.
There be the caves where Elpha he imprisoned underground.
And they left San Estévan, on their right that lay afar.
Within the woods of Corpes, the Heirs of Carrión are.
And high the hills are wooded, to the clouds the branches sweep,
And savage are the creatures that roundabout them creep;
And there upon a bower with a clear spring they light
And there the Heirs of Carrión bade that their tent be pight.
There with their men about them, that night they lay at rest.

With their wives clasped to their bosom their affection they protest,
But ill the twain fulfilled it, when the dawn came up the East.
They bade put goods a plenty on the back of every beast.
Where they at night found lodging, now have they struck the tent.
The people of their household far on before them went.
Of the two Heirs of Carrión so the commandment ran,
That none behind should linger, a woman or a man.
But Dame Sol and Dame Elvíra their wives shall tarry still,
With whom it is their pleasure to dally to their fill.

The others have departed. They four are left alone.
Great evil had been plotted by the Heirs of Carrión.
"Dame Sol and Dame Elvíra, ye may take this for true:
Here in the desert wildwood shall a mock be made of you.
Today is our departure, we will leave you here behind.
And in the lands of Carrión no portion shall you find.
Let them hasten with these tidings to the Cid Campeador.
Thus, the matter of the lion, we avenge ourselves therefor."

Their furs and their mantles, from the ladies they have whipped.
In their shifts and their tunics they left the ladies stripped.
With spur on heel before them those wicked traitors stand,
And saddle-girths both stout and strong they have taken in the hand.
When the ladies had beheld it, then out spake Sol the dame:
"Don Diégo, don Ferrándo, we beeech you in God's name.
You have two swords about you, that for strength and edge are known.
And one they call Coláda, the other is Tizón.
Strike off our heads together, and martyrs we shall die.
The Moriscos and the Christians against this deed shall cry.
It stands not with our deserving that we should suffer thus.
So evil an example, then do not make of us.
Unto our own abasement, if you scourge us, you consent,
That men will bring against you in parle and parliament."

Naught profits it the ladies, however hard they pray.
And now the Heirs of Carrión upon them 'gan to lay.
With the buckled girths they scourged them in fashion unbeseen,
And exceeding was their anguish from the sharp spurs and keen.
They rent the shifts and wounded the bodies of the two,
And forth upon the tunics the clear blood trickled through.
In their very hearts the ladies have felt that agony.
What a fair fortune were it, if God's will it might be,
Had then appeared before them the Cid the Campeador.

Powerless were the ladies, and the brothers scourged them sore.

Their shifts and their sullies throughout the blood did stain.
Of scourging the two ladies wearied the brothers twain,

Which man should smite most fiercely they had vied each with each.
Dame Sol and Dame Elvíra had no longer power of speech.
Within the wood of Corpes for dead they left the pair.

CXXIX.

Their cloaks and furs of ermine along with them they bare,
In their shifts and tunics, fainting, they left them there behind,
A prey to every wild-fowl and beast of savage kind.

Know you, for dead, not living, they left them in such cheer.
Good hap it were if now the Cid, Roy Diaz, should appear.

CXXX.

The Heirs of Carrión for dead have left them thus arrayed,
For the one dame to the other, could give no sort of aid.
They sang each other's praises as they journeyed through the wood:
"For the question of our marriage we have made our vengeance good.
Unbesought, to be our lemans we should not take that pair,
Because as wedded consorts for our arms unfit they were.
For the insult of the lion vengeance shall thus be ta'en."

CXXXI.

They sang each other's praises, the Heirs of Carrión twain.
But now of Felez Múñoz will I tell the tale once more.
Even he that was nephew to the Cid Campeador.
They had bidden him ride onward, but he was not well content.
And his heart smote within him as along the road he went.
Straightway from all the others' a space did he withraw.
There Felez Múñoz entered into a thick-grown straw,
Till the coming of his cousins should be plain to be perceived
Or what the Heirs of Carrión as at that time achieved.
And he beheld them coming, and heard them say their say,
But they did not espy him, nor thought of him had they.
Be it known death he had not scaped, had they on him laid eye.
And the two Heirs rode onward, pricking fast the spur they ply.
On their trail Felez Múñoz has turned him back again.
He came upon his cousins. In a swoon lay the twain.
And crying "Oh my cousins!" straightway did he alight.
By the reins the horse he tethered, and went to them forthright.

"Dame Sol and Dame Elvíra, cousins of mine that be,
The two Heirs of Carrión have borne them dastardly.
Please God that for this dealing they may get a shameful gain."
And straightway he bestirred him to life to bring the twain.
Deep was their swoon. Of utterance all power they had forlorn.
Of his heart the very fabric thereby in twain was torn.
"Oh my cousins Dame Elvíra and Dame Sol," he cried and spake,
"For the love of the Creator, my cousins twain, awake,
While yet the day endureth, ere falls the evening-hour,
Lest in the wood our bodies the savage beast devour."

In Dame Sol and Dame Elvíra fresh life began to rise;
And they looked on Felez Múñoz when at last they oped their eyes:
"For the love of God my cousins, now be of courage stout.
From the time the Heirs of Carrión shall miss me from their rout,
With utmost speed thereafter will they hunt me low and high.
And if God will not help us, in this place we then must die."
To him out spoke the Lady Sol in bitter agony:
"If the Campeador, our father, deserveth well of thee,
My cousin give us water, so may God help thee too."
A hat had Felez Múñoz, from Valencia, fine and new,
Therein he caught the water, and to his cousins bore.
To drink their fill he gave them, for they were stricken sore.
Till they rose up, most earnestly he begged them and implored.
He comforts them and heartens them until they are restored.
He took the two and quickly set them a-horse again.
He wrapped them in his mantle. He took the charger's rein
Aud sped them on, and through Corpes Wood they took their way.
They issued from the forest between the night and day.
The waters of Duéro they at the last attain.
At Dame Urráca's tower he left behind the twain,
And then unto Saint Stephen's did Felez Múñoz fare.
He found Diégo Tellez, Alvar Fañez' vassal, there.
When he had heard those tidings on his heart great sorrow fell.
And he took beasts of burden and garments that excel.
Dame Sol and Dame Elvíra to welcome did he go.
He lodged the in Saint Stephen's. Great honor did he show
Those ladies. In Saint Stephen's very gentle are the men,
When they had heard the tidings their hearts were sorry then.
To the Cid's daughters tribute of plenteous fare they yield.
In that place the ladies tarried, till the time when they were healed.

Loud they sang each other's praises, those Heirs of Carrión,
And of their deeds the tidings through all these lands were known.
Of the good King don Alfonso the heart for grief was torn.

To Valencia the city now are the tidings borne.
To my lord Cid the Campeador that message when they brought,
Thereon for a full hour's space, he pondered and he thought.
His hand he has uplifted and gripped his beard amain:
"Now unto Christ be glory who o'er all the earth doth reign.
Since thus sought they of Carrión to keep mine honor whole.
Now by this beard that never was plucked by living soul,
Thereby the Heirs of Carrión no pleasure shall they gain.
As for the dames my daughters, I shall marry well the twain.

The Cid and all his courtiers were sorry grievously,
Heart and soul Alvar Fañez a sad man was he.
Minaya with Per Vermudóz straightway the steed bestrode,
And good Martin Antolínez in Burgos that abode,
With ten score horse that to that end the Cid set in array.
Most earnestly he charged them to ride both night and day,
And to the town Valencia his daughters twain to bring.
About their lord's commandment there was no tarrying.
Swiftly they got on horseback and rode both day and night.
Into Gormaz they entered, a strong place of might.
In sooth one night they lodged there. To Saint Stephen's tidings flew
That Minaya was come thither to bring home his cousins two.
The dwellers in Saint Stephen's, as becomes the true and brave,
To Minaya and his henchmen a noble welcome gave,
And for tribute to Minaya brought that night of cheer good store.
He desired not to accept it, but he thanked them well therefor;
"Thanks, stout men of Saint Stephen's, for ye bear you wise and well.
For the honor that ye did us, for the thing that us befel,
Where bides the Cid the Campeador he gives true thanks to you,
As I do here. May God on high give you your payment due."

Therewith they thanked him greatly, with him were all content
Then swiftly to their lodging to rest that night they went.
Where bode his kin, Minaya to see them went his ways. Dame
Sol and Dame Elvíra upon him fixed their gaze: "So heartily we
thank thee, as our eyes on God were set,
And prithee thank Him for it, since we are living yet.
In the days of ease thereafter, in Valencia when we dwell,
The tale of our affliction, we shall have strength to tell.

CXXXII.

The dames and Alvar Fañez, the tears flowed from their eyes.
Per Vermudóz because of them was sorely grieved likewise.
"Dame Sol and Dame Elvíra, be not down-hearted still,
Since you are well and living and without other ill.
Ye have lost a good marriage, better matches shall ye make.
Oh may we soon behold the day when vengeance we shall take!"
So all that night they lay there keeping a merry tide.
The next day in the morning they fettled them to ride.
The people of Saint Stephen's their party escort bore,
With every sort of solace e'en to Riodamor.
There they took leave, and got them in stead to travel back.
Minaya and the ladies rode forward on the track.
They have passed Alcoceva. On the right Gormaz left they.
They have come o'er the river in the place called Vadorrey,
And in the town Berlanga their lodging have they made.
The next day in the morning set forth the cavalcade.
In the place called Medína their shelter have they sought.
From Medína to Molína on the next day were they brought.
And there the Moor Avengalvón was pleased in heart thereby.
Forth with good will he issued to give them welcome high,
For my lord Cid's love a supper he gave them rich and great.
Thence on unto Valencia they have departed straight.
When to him who in good honor was born the news of it was sent,
Swiftly he got on horseback, and forth to greet them went.
As he rode he brandished weapons; very joyful was his face.
My lord the Cid came forward his daughters to embrace.
And after he had kissed them he smiled upon the two:
"Are ye then come my daughters? 'Gainst ill God succor you.
This marriage I accepted, daring not say otherwise.
May the Creator grant it, who dwelleth in the skies,
That you with better husbands hereafter I may see.
God! on my sons of Carrión grant me avenged to be.
"The hands of their father to kiss, the two bent down.
And under arms they hastened and came into the town.
Their mother Dame Xiména with them good cheer she made.
And he who in good hour was born, he tarried not nor stayed,
But there unto his comrades so privily he spake:
To King Alfonso of Castile those tidings shall they take.

CXXXIII.

"Where art thou, Muño Gustióz, vassal of fair report
In a good time I cherished and reared thee in my court.
To King Alfonso in Castile these tidings do thou take.
His hands with heart and spirit do thou kiss them for my sake—
I am known for his vassal, he for my lord is known—
At the dishonor done me by the heirs of Carrión
Shall the good King be troubled in his soul and in his heart.
He gave to wed my daughters, therein I had no part.
Since my girls they have deserted with great dishonor thus,
If they have put an insult by that action upon us,
The great part and the little, my lord's is all the scorn.
My possessions, which are mighty, off with them have they borne,
This and the other insult well may make me ill content.
Bring them to parley with me in assize or parliament,
So that I may have justice on the heirs of Carrión,
For in my heart the anguish exceeding great is grown."

Thereupon Muño Gustióz swiftly the steed bestrode.
To wait upon his pleasure two horsemen with him rode,
And with him were esquires that of his household were.
They departed from Valencia as fast as they could spur,
They gave themselves no respite either by night or noon.
And the King don Alfonso he found at Sahagún.
Of Castile is he the ruler, of León furthermore.
And likewise of Asturias, yea, to San Salvador.
As far as Santiago for lord paramount is he known.
The counts throughout Galicia him for their sovereign own.
As soon as Muño Gustióz got down from horseback there,
Before the Saints he kneeled him, and to God he made his prayer.
Where the court was in the palace straightway his steps he bent.
The horsemen two that served him as their lord beside him went.
As soon as they had entered amid the royal train
The King saw them and knew lightly Muño Gustióz again.
The King rose up and nobly he welcomed him and well.
before the King Alfonso on bended knee he fell.
The King's feet, Muño Gustióz, that wight, has kissed withal:
"A boon, King, thee the sovereign of kingdoms broad they call.
The Campeador, he kisses so well thy feet and hands;
Thou art his lord; thy vassal as at all times he stands.
To Carrión's Heirs his daughters were given to wed by thee.
It was a glorious marriage for it was thy decree.
The honor that befel us is to thee already known,
What flout was put upon us by the Heirs of Carrión.

Fiercely they scourged the daughters of the Cid Campeador.
Naked, in great dishonor and from the scourging sore,
In Corpes Wood unguarded they cast the dames away,
Unto the savage creatures and the forest-fowl a prey,
And lo! now to Valencia his daughters are restored.
For this thy hand he kisses as a vassal to his lord,
That thou bring them to confront him in assize or parliament.
He holds himself dishonored, but fouler art thou shent.
And King, sore should it grieve thee, and he prays, for wise art thou,
That my lord Cid may have justice on the Heirs of Carrión now."
The king long while was silent, pondering thereon apart:
"The truth will I say to thee. It grieves me to the heart.
So hast thou, Muño Gustióz, herein a true thing said,
For to Carrión's Heirs, his daughters I gave indeed to wed.
For good I did it, deeming that there his vantage lay.
But would now that that marriage had ne'er been made today.
My lord the Cid and I myself, sore grieved at heart are we.
I must help him unto justice, so God my savior be.
Though I would not at this season, I must do even so.
And now through all my Kingdom forth shall mine heralds go,
For in Toledo city a court shall they proclaim,
So that counts may come and nobles that be of lesser name.
The Heirs of Carrión thither I will summon furthermore;
And there shall they give justice to my lord Cid Campeador.
Yet while I can prevent it, he shall have no cause to mourn.

CXXXIV.

"And say unto the Campeador, who in good hour was born,
That he may with his vassals for these seven weeks prepare
To come unto Toledo. That term I grant him fair.
I will hold these assizes since the Cid to me is dear.
Greet them all for me fairly, let them be of joyful cheer.
For what befel, of honor they yet shall have no lack."
His leave ta'en, Muño Gustióz to my lord Cid turned back.
Since he had undertaken that the charge on him should fall,
Alfonso the Castilian delayed it not at all.
To León and Santiago he sent letters without fail,
And unto the Galicians, and the men of Portingale.
Tidings to them in Carrión and in Castile they bring
Of a Court held in Toledo by the much honored King,
And that there they should be gathered when seven weeks should end.
Who stayed at home, true vassalage no longer could pretend.
And all men so determined throughout his breadth of lands
Not to fail in the fulfillment of the King's high commands.

CXXXV.

Now are the Heirs of Carrión troubled by the report
That the King within Toledo was about to hold his court.
They fear my lord Cid Campeador will have his part therein,
And they took counsel, seeing that they were near of kin.
The King for dispensation to stay from court they prayed.
Said the King:
"I will not do it, as God shall stand mine aid.
For my lord Cid the Campeador that place shall come unto,
And you shall do him justice for he makes complaint of you.
Who refuses, or denies it to come unto mine assize,
Let him quit my realm. The fellow finds no favor in mine eyes."

And now the Heirs of Carrión saw that it must be done
Since they are very near of kin, counsel they took thereon.
Count García that to ruin the Cid sought evermore,
My lord the Cid's arch-foeman, share in these matters bore.
This man has given counsel to the Heirs of Carrión twain.
Time came: to the assizes to hasten they were fain.
Thither among the foremost doth good King Alfonso go,
With him the Count don Henry, and Count don Remónd also—
For the sire of the most noble the Emperor was he known.
There came the Count don Froíla and the Count don Birbón.
Out of his realm came many of wise hearts and leal
All the best men were gathered of the kingdom of Castile.
And there with Crespo de Grañón, Count don García came
And he who ruled in Oca—Alvar Diaz was his name.
With Gonzalvo Ansuórez, Ansuór Gonzálvez stood.
Know ye well with them was Pero of the Ansuórez blood.
Diégo and Ferrándo both to the place resort,
And with them a great company that they had brought to Court.
Upon my lord Cid Campeador 'tis their intent to fall.
Unto the place they gather from every side and all.
But he who in good hour was born, not yet hath he drawn nigh.
Because so long he tarries is the king displeased thereby.
My lord the Cid the Campeador is come on the fifth day.
He has sent Alvar Fañez ahead of his array,
That he might kiss the King his hands that is his lord of right,
The King might know it surely, he would be at hand that night.
Now when the King had heard it, his heart was glad indeed.
With companies most mighty the King leaped on the steed,
And him who in good hour was born he went to welcome there.
Came the Cid and all his henchmen equipped exceeding fair.
Oh! noble troops that follow a captain of such might!

When good King don Alfonso of my lord the Cid got sight,
My lord the Cid, the Campeador, cast himself on the sward.
Himself he thus could humble and do honor to his lord.
When the King saw he tarried not.
"Saint Isidore to speed!
This day so shalt thou never. Mount, Cid, upon the steed!
If not, so ends my pleasure. Let us greet on either part
With heart and soul. What grieveth thee hath hurt me to the heart.
God ordereth that by thee the court this day shall honored be."
My lord Cid, the true Campeador, to this "Amen" said he.
He kissed his hand and fairly gave him greeting then:
"To God now thanks be given, that I see thee, lord, again.
To thee I bow, so also to Count don Remónd I bow,
To Count Henry and to all men that are in presence now.
God save our friends and foremost, sire, may he cherish thee.
My wife the Dame Xiména—a worthy dame is she—
Kisses thy hands. My daughters, the twain do so as well,
That so thou mayst have pity for the ill thing that befel."
"Verily, so God help me," answered the King thereto.

CXXXVI.

Then homeward to Toledo, the King returned anew.
Unfain to cross the Tagus was my lord Cid that night:
"A boon, King. The Creator, may he shield thee in His might!
Oh sire, do thou get ready to enter in the town.
In San Serván my henchman and I will lay us down,
For hither in the night-tide shall come those bands of mine;
And I will keep my vigil here by the holy shrine.
I will come to town tomorrow at the breaking of the day,
And, ere I eat my dinner, to court will take my way."
To him the King gave answer: "Surely, I am content."
Then the King don Alfonso into Toledo went.
My lord the Cid Roy Diaz lieth in San Serván.
To make candles and to set them on the shrine, his order ran.
To watch that sanctuary was gladness to his heart,
As he prayed to the Creator and spake to him apart.
Minaya, and as many as were gathered of good fame
Were in accord together when at length the morning came.

CXXXVII.

Matins and prime they sang there till the dawn had begun,
Before the sun had risen the mass was o'er and done.
With rich and timely offering that chapel they endow.

"Minaya Alvar Fañez—my strongest arm art thou—
Thyself shall hear me company and the Bishop, don Jerome
So too this Muño Gustióz and Per Vermudóz shall come,
And Martin Antolínez from Burgos true and tried
And with Alvar Salvadórez, Alvar Alvarez beside,
And Martin Múñoz who was born in a season of good grace,
So likewise Felez Múñoz a nephew of my race.
Mal Anda wise exceeding, along with me shall go
And the good Galínd Garcíaz of Aragon also.
With these knights a round hundred of the good men here ordain.
Let all men wear their tunics the harness to sustain,
Let them assume the hauberks that white as sunlight glare,
And upon the hauberks ermines and mantles of the vair
Let them lace tight their armour, let not the arms be seen.
They shall bear beneath their mantles the swords both sweet and keen.
To the court in such a fashion to enter am I fain,
My rights there to demand them and to speak my meaning plain.
If there the Heirs of Carrión seek to dishonor me,
No whit then shall I fear them, though a hundred strong they be."
To him all gave their answer: "Such, lord, is our desire,"
Even as he had commanded they ordered their attire.
He who in happy hour was born would brook no more delay.
Upon his legs the hosen of fair cloth he drew straightway,
And shoes adorned most richly upon his feet has done;
he donned a shirt of linen fine as white as is the sun;
The sleeves are laced, moreover, with gold and silver braid.
The cuff fit close upon them for he bade them so be made.
Thereo'er a silken tunic most fairly wrought he drew.
The threads of gold shone brightly that were woven through and
   through.
A red fur gown gold-belted he cast his tunic o'er.
That gown alway he weareth, my lord Cid Campeador.
He hath of finest linen a cap upon his hair,
With the gold wrought, moreover, and fashioned with due care,
That the locks of the good Campeador might not be disarrayed.
And with a cord his mighty beard my lord the Cid doth braid.
All this he did desiring well his person to dispose.
O'er his attire a mantle of mighty worth he throws.
Thereat might all men wonder that thereabouts did stand.
Then with the chosen hundred whereto he gave command
From San Serván forth issuing he got to horse apace.
Under arms the Cid departed unto the judgment-place.
Duly without the postern he descended from his horse,
And prudently he entered the palace with his force.
Midmost he went; his hundred girt him round on every side.

When they had seen him enter, who was born in happy tide,
Then the good King Alfonso upon his feet did rise,
So also Count don Henry, and Count don Remónd likewise.
And they arose, the others of the court, ye well may know.
To him who in good hour was born great honor did they show.
One man there was arose not—'twas Crespo de Grañón—
Nor any of the party of the Heirs of Carrión.

The King has ta'en my lord Cid's hand:
"Come sit thee, Campeador,
On the bench here beside me—thy gift to me of yore.
Thou art our better, though there be umbrage therefor that take."
Then he who won Valencia for gratitude he spake:
"Sit like a king and master on thy bench, for it is thine;
In this station will I tarry here with these men of mine."

Of what my lord Cid uttered was the King's heart glad and fain.
Upon a bench well carven the Cid his seat has ta'en;
The hundred men that guard him are seated round him there.
And all men in the Cortes upon my lord Cid stare,
And the long beard he weareth that is braided with a cord.
He seems by his apparel to be a splendid lord.
For shame the Heirs of Carrión his gaze they could not meet.
The good King don Alfonso then rose unto his feet:
"Hearken ye gentle companies, so God your hands sustain.
But two court have I holden in the space of all my reign.
In Burgos one, in Carrión the next did I array;
The third here in Toledo have I come to hold today,
For the Cid's love, whose birth-hour for a glad time is known,
That so he may have justice on the Heirs of Carrión.
Let all men know they did him a bitter injury.
The Counts Remónd and Henry judges thereof shall be,
And all you counts, moreover, in the feud who bear no part.
In your minds turn it over, for ye are wise of heart.
See that ye render justice. All falseness I gainsay.
On one side and the other let us keep the peace this day.
Who breaks our peace, I swear it by the Saint Isidore
Shall be banished from my kingdom, nor have my favor more.
His side I will maintain it whose cause is right and fair.
Therefore let the Cid Campeador forthwith his suit declare.
Then shall we hear what Carrión's Heirs in answer shall depose."

My lord Cid kissed the King his hand. Then to his feet he rose:
"My sovereign and my master great thanks I give to thee
That thou this court hast summoned out of pure love for me.

Against the Heirs of Carrión this matter I reclaim.
They cast away my daughters. I had thereby no shame,
For thou gavest them in marriage. What deed to do today
Thou know'st well. From Valencia when they took my girls away,
I loved with heart and spirit the Heirs of Carrión,
And the two swords I gave them, Coláda and Tizón—
I won them in such manner as a good knight became—
That they might do you service and do honor to their fame.
When in the Wood of Corpes they left my girls forlorn,
They lost my love forever, for they made of me a scorn.
Since my sons-in-law they are not, let them give me either sword."
"All of the claim is righteous," so the judges gave accord.

Then said Count don García: "Of this let us debate."
Apart from the assizes went the Heirs of Carrión straight,
And all their following with them and the kindred of their name.
And swiftly they debated, and to their resolve they came:
"Now the Cid Campeador for us doth a great favor do,
Since for his girls' dishonor for no damage doth he sue.
With the King don Alfonso, we soon shall be at one.
The swords them let us give him, for so the suit is done;
They will hold the court no longer, when he has the swords once more.
From us no further justice for the Cid Campeador."
That parley being over, to court they get them now.

"Thy favor, King Alfonso, our overlord art thou.
And we cannot deny it, for he gave us the two brands.
And since that we return them he desires now and demands,
Into his hand to give them in thy presence are we fain."
Then they brought forth Coláda and Tizón, the falchions twain,
Straightway they gave them over to the King their sovereign's hands.
The whole court shone glorious when they brought forth the brands.
The pommels and the hilt-bars are all of massy gold;
To the true henchmen of the court 'twas a marvel to behold.
The King my lord Cid summoned, to him the swords he gave.
His sovereign's hands he kisseth. He receiveth either glaive.
To the bench whence he had risen, he turned him back again,
And in his hands he held them, he looked upon the twain.
Changelings they could not give him; he knew the two aright,
And his heart laughed within him, he was filled with all delight.
"Now by my beard none ever plucked," gripping it hard he spake,
For Dame Sol and Dame Elvíra high vengeance I will take."

By name his nephew Pero he has called out before;
And stretching forth his hand, to him the sword Tizón gave o'er.

"Take it nephew. The sword's master now is fairer of renown."
To good Martin Antolínez the man of Burgos town,
Stretching forth his hand Coláda into his care he gave;

"Thou Martin Antolínez, who art a vassal brave,
Take Coláda that I captured from a true knight without fail,
From him of Barcelona, from Remónd Berenguél.
That thou mayst guard it rightly, therefore I give it thee,
I know if aught befall thee, if occasion e'er should be,
Great fame and estimation with the sword shalt thou attain."
The lord Cid's hands he kissed them. He took the sword again.

My lord the Cid the Campeador unto his feet rose he;
"Now thanks to the Creator and my lord the King to thee.
With the swords Coláda and Tizón I am content indeed,
But I have a farther issue 'gainst Carrión Heirs to plead:
When with them from Valencia my daughters twain they bore,
Three thousand marks of silver and gold I gave them o'er.
When I did this, the winning of all their end they saw.
Let them restore the treasure. They are not my sons-in-law."

Now might you hearken Carrión's Heirs, what a complaint made they.
To them said the Count don Remónd: "Give answer, 'Yea' or 'Nay'!",
And then the Heirs of Carrión, they made their answer plain:
"Therefore to the Cid Campeador we gave his swords again
That he might demand naught further, for his suit is closed thereby."
Then straightway the Count don Remónd unto them made reply:
"This say we: With the pleasure of the Sovereign if it stands,
You shall give satisfaction in what the Cid demands."
The good King said: "The measure with my assent doth meet."
And now hath the Cid Campeador arisen to his feet:

"Say of those goods I gave you, will ye give them me anew
Or render an accounting?"

Then Carrión's Heirs withdrew.
For the greatness of that treasure they could not as one consent,
And the two Heirs of Carrión the whole of it had spent.
They returned with their decision, and spake their pleasure thus:
"The Captor of Valencia, he presses sore on us.
Since lust for our possession so on him hand hath laid,
From our estates in Carrión the money shall be paid."

And then outspake the judges since the debt the Heirs avowed:
"If it be the Cid's desire, it is not disallowed.

So we ordain, for such wise with our pleasure doth it sort,
That ye repay it to him in this place before the court."

Out spake the King Alfonso when their words were at an end:
"The inward of this lawing we wholly comprehend,
That justice is demanded by the Cid Campeador.
Now of those marks three thousand, I have in hand tenscore;
They were given to me duly by the Heirs of Carrión twain.
Since so sore are they impoverished, I will give it them again.
To the Cid born in fair hour, let them pay the money back.
To pay their debt, that money I will not let them lack."

As for Ferránd Gonzálvez, what he said ye now shall hear:
"We have in our possession no minted goods and gear."

To him then the Count don Remónd answered to this intent:
"All of the gold and silver, the twain of you have spent.
Before the King Alfonso, our verdict we proclaim,
That ye pay in goods. The Campeador, let him accept the same."

Now saw the Heirs of Carrión what need must be their course.
Ye might have seen led thither full many a swift horse,
Many fat mules, moreover, and many a well-paced jade,
And every sort of armour, and many a fine blade.
My lord the Cid accepted even as the court assessed,
Beyond the tenscore marks whereof Alfonso stood possessed,
To him who in good hour was born the Heirs have paid the price.
On others' goods they borrow, for their own will not suffice
Know well for fools men took them, from that suit when 'scaped the
  twain.

CXXXVIII.

All of those great possessions my lord the Cid has ta'en.
The men keep all that treasure, and they will ward it well.
When this was done, a-pondering on other things they fell:

Lord King, for love of charity, a further favor yet,
Of my complaints the chiefest, I cannot now forget.
Let the whole court now hear me, and have pity on my woe:
As for these Heirs of Carrión, the which have shamed me so,
I brook not that unchallenged they may go hence away.

CXXXIX.

"In what thing I affronted you, ye Heirs of Carrión say,
In what fashion whatsoever, in earnest or in sport.
Let me make amends according to the judgment of the court.
Why did ye tear in tatters the fabric of my heart?
With great honor from Valencia what time ye did depart,
I gave to you my daughters, and besides great wealth and gear.
Now say, ye dogs and traitors, since ye did not hold them dear,
Why took ye from Valencia what was their dower of right,
And wherefore with the girth and spur the ladies did ye smite?
Alone in Corpes Forest ye cast the twain away,
Unto the savage creatures and the wood-fowl for a prey.
In all ye did unto them, like vile men did ye show.
Let the Court judge; satisfaction shall I get therefor or no?"

CXL.

And lo! Count don García has risen up amain:
"Let us now have thy favor, best of all kings in Spain.
Of the courts proclaimed is now the Cid well versed in the affairs.
Since he let it wax so mighty, 'tis a long beard he wears.
Some he affrights and others are for fear in sorry case.
But as for them of Carrión, theirs is a lofty race,
His daughters e'en as lemans to love becomes them not.
Who to them for lawful consorts those ladies would allot?
When they cast them off, then did they as might the right befit.
All things he says soever we value not a whit."

And thereupon the Campeador his beard in hand gripped he:
"To God who ruleth Heaven and the whole Earth glory be.
Since tenderly I kept it, is my beard grown so long.
Count, say what is the reason, that thou dost my beard this wrong,
That since its first growth ever has been so gently reared.
No man born of woman has ever plucked that beard.
Nor has son of Moor or Christian e'er torn that beard of mine,
As once in Cabra Castle I did, oh Count, to thine,
When at one time on Cabra and thy beard my hand I set.
Not a lad but for the plucking his pinch thereof could get.
Nor is it yet grown even what portion I did tear.
Here hidden in my wallet those tokens yet I bear."

CXLI.

Now had Ferránd Gonzálvez risen to his feet that tide.
What thing ye now shall hearken that there so loud he cried:

"Cid, do thou now give over the suit which thou hast made,
For the whole of thy possession into thine hands is paid.
Look that thou make not greater the feud twixt us and thee,
For the two Counts of Carrión by lineage are we.
Of kings' and emperors' daughters are we fit to win the hands;
To wed the girls of little chiefs scarce with our lineage stands.
When thy daughters we abandoned we did but what was right.
Not worse therefor but better, are we then in our own sight."

CXLII.

To Per Vermudóz Roy Diaz my lord the Cid looked now:
"Speak then, good Pero Mudo, though a silent man art thou.
The ladies are my daughters, thy cousins twain are they.
Into thy teeth they cast it, when such a thing they say.
Thou shalt not do this battle, if I the answer make.

CXLIII.

And thereupon Per Vermudóz began the tale and spake.
No words he utters clearly, for 'tis a tongue-halt man.
Natheless no rest he gave them, be it known, when he began:
"To thee, Cid, now I tell it, for such thy customs be,
That in Court, Pero Mudo, ever thou callest me.
And verily thou knowest that I can do no more.
As for what I must accomplish, there shall be no lack therefore.

"What thing thou saidest soever, Ferrándo, was a lie.
Through the Campeador thy glory was risen yet more high.
I can relate unto thee thine every trick and sleight.
Minds't thou, near high Valencia, what time we fought the fight?
Thou didst of the true Campeador for the first onslaught pray.
And there a Moor thou sawest, whom thou wentest forth to slay.
Or e'er thou camest to him, before him didst thou flee.
If aid I had not borne thee, he had roughly handled thee.
But I rushed on beyond thee, and with the Moor did close,
And I made that Moor flee backward at the foremost of my blows.
To thee I gave his charger, and kept the thing concealed.
Until this day that cowardice I never have revealed.

Before the Cid and all men thine own praises didst thou sing,
How thou slewest the Morisco, and didst a gallant thing.
And they believed it of thee, knowing not the truth at all.
Of thy person art thou handsome, but thy courage it is small,
Tongue without hands, the manhood to speak where gottest thou?

CXLIV.

"Do thou say on, Ferrándo. That my words are truth avow:
That matter of the lion in Valencia dost thou keep
In mind still, when he burst his bonds while the Cid lay asleep?
Ferrándo, then what didst thou, when thy terror overbore?
Thou didst thrust thyself behind the bench of the Cid Campeador.
Thou didst hide, Ferrándo, wherefore cheap today thy worth is found,
But we to guard our master his pallet gathered round,
Till he who won Valencia out of his sleep did wake.
He rose up from the pallet, at the lion did he make.
His head the lion bended, for the Cid the beast did wait.
By the neck he let himself be ta'en. In the cage he thrust him straight.
When came once more the Campeador, there he saw his vassals stand.
He asked about his sons-in-law, but neither found at hand.
For a wicked man and traitor thy person I arraign.
In fight before Alfonso that same I will maintain,
For Dame Sol and Dame Elvíra, for the Cid's daughters' sake.
Thou didst cast away the ladies thine honor cheap to make.
Ye are men to all appearance, tender women are those two;
Yet in every way whatever they are worthier than you.
If, when we join the combat, God shall like well in his heart,
Thyself shalt thou confess it, like a traitor as thou art.
Whatever I have uttered shall then be known for true."
And thereupon was ending of speech between these two.

CXLV.

And Dídago Gonzálvez what he uttered ye shall hear:
"We twain are Counts by lineage of blood of the most clear.
Such marriages in no way we twain would undertake,
With my lord Cid don Rodrigo alliance for to make.
We do not yet repent us that we put his daughters by:
So long as life endureth, may they sigh many a sigh.
A sore reproach upon them what we did will still remain.
The same with utmost valor in the fight will I maintain:
When we cast away the women we made our honor good."

CXLVI.

Then Martin Antolínez upon his feet he stood:
Thou wretch, do thou keep silence. Mouth that truth knoweth not!
The matter of the lion hast thou so soon forgot
Out through the door thou fleddest lurking in the court outside,
Behind the wine-press timber in that hour didst thou hide.
That mantle and that tunic were worn no more by thee.
In fight I will maintain it. No other can it be.
Since the lord Cid his daughters forth in such plight ye threw,
They are in every fashion far worthier shall you.
At the ending of the combat then thine own mouth shall avow
That lies are all thine utterance, and a traitor knave art thou."

CXLVII.

Between those two the parley has come unto an end.
Now did Ansuór Gonzálvez into the palace wend.
Was an ermine cloak about him, and his tunic trailed behind.
His countenance was ruddy, for but lately had he dined.
In what he had to utter small discretion did he show:

CXLVIII.

"How now ye noble gentlemen, was ever such a woe?
With Bivár's lord Cid such honor who would have thought to find?
On the Ovirna water his millstones let him grind,
And take his wonted toll-corn. Would any man have thought
That with the Heirs of Carrión alliances he sought?"

CXLIX.

And then did Muño Gustióz rise to his feet forthright:
"Thou wretch, do thou keep silent! Thou wicked traitor wight!
Before to prayers thou goest, certain thou art to dine.
Whoe'er in peace thou kissest, sickens at that belch of thine.
Whether to friend or master thou speakest perjury,
False unto all, and falsest to the God who fashioned thee!
And never in thy friendship will I have any part,
And I will make thee say it that what I say thou art."

Said now the King Alfonso: "Let the suit quiet lie.
Who have challenged shall do battle, so help me the Most High."

Soon as the suit was finished to the court two horsemen came,

And Inigo Ximénez and Ojárra men them name;
For Navarra's Heir-apparent, proxy-suitor was the one,
The other was the suitor for the Heir of Aragon.
And there the twain together have kissed Alfonso's hand,
The Cid Campeador his daughters in marriage they demand,
Of the realms Navarre and Aragon the lady-queens to be.
May he send them with his blessing and with all courtesy.
Thereat the whole court listened, and stillness fell them o'er.
Upon his feet rose straightway my lord Cid Campeador:
"A boon, Oh King Alfonso, my sovran lord thou art.
For this to the Creator very thankful is my heart,
Since both Navarre and Aragon have made request so high.
Thou didst give to wed my daughters before. It was not I.
Here then behold my daughters, the twain are in thine hand.
With them I will do nothing, except at thy command."
The King rose up. For silence in the court the word he gave:
"I beg it of thee, Campeador, the true Cid and the brave,
That hereto thou yield agreement. I will grant the thing this day:
And it shall be consented in open court straightway,
For so will grow thy glory and shine honor and thy lands."
Now is the Cid arisen. He kissed Alfonso's hands:
"To whatever thing shall please thee, I give consent, my lord."
Then said the King: "God grant thee an excellent reward!
To Inigo Ximénez and Ojárra, to you two,
I yield my full permission for this marriage unto you,
That Dame Sol and Dame Elvíra, who the Cid's daughters are,
Wed, one the Heir of Aragon, and the other of Navarre.
May he yield his girls with blessings in an honorable way."

Then Inigo Ximénez and Ojárra, up rose they,
And the hands of Don Alfonso in that hour kissed again.
The hands of the Cid Campeador thereafter kissed the twain,
And there their faith they plighted, and solemn oaths they swore,
That they would fulfill entirely what they promised or yet more.
Because of this were many in the court exceeding glad;
But the two Heirs of Carrión, therein no joy they had.

Minaya Alvar Fañez upon his feet rose he:
"As from my King and Master I beg a boon of thee,
And let it not be grievous to the Cid Campeador.
I have through these assizes kept my peace heretofore,
But now to utter somewhat for mine own part fain am I."
Said the King: "Now all my spirit, it is well pleased thereby.
Say on! Say on, Minaya, what to thy heart is dear."

"You in the court, I beg you to my word to lend an ear.
'Gainst Carrión's Heirs needs must I now a charge most mighty bring:
I gave to them my cousins by Alfonso's hand, the King.
With blessings and with honor they took them in their care.
The Cid Campeador he gave them most rich possessions there.
They cast away those ladies, for all that we were loth.
For wicked men and traitors I make challenge of you both.
From the great sons of Gomez does your lineage come down,
Whence many counts have issued of valor and renown,
But this day all to certainly their cunning do we learn.
For this to the Creator, now thanks do I return,
That of Navarre and Aragon the Heirs in marriage sue
For Dame Sol and Elvíra that are my cousins two.
Erst for true wives ye had them, who now their hands shall kiss
And call them Dame, though sorely ye take the thing amiss.
Praise to our God in Heaven and our lord the King therefor.
So greatly grows the honor of the Cid my Campeador.
In every way soever ye are even as I say.
Is there any in the presence to reply or say me nay?
Lo! I am Alvar Fañez, against the most of might!"

And thereupon did Gomez Peláez stand upright:
"Say of what worth, Minaya, is this ye speak so free?
For here in the assizes are men enough for thee.
Who otherwise would have it, it would ruin him indeed.
If it be perchance God's pleasure that our quarrel well should speed,
Then well shalt thou see whether or right or wrong ye were."
Said the King: "The suit is over. No further charge prefer.
Tomorrow is the combat; at the rising of the sun
By the three who challenged with thee in the court it shall be done."

Thereon the Heirs of Carrión have spoken presently:
"Lord King, a season grant us for tomorn it cannot be.
We have given to the Campeador our arms and many a steed,
First to our land of Carrión to go we have sore need."
And then the King had spoken to the Campeador again:
"Where thou shalt bid, this combat, let it be underta'en.
"My lord, I will not do it," my lord the Cid said he,
"More than the lands of Carrión Valencia liketh me."

To him the King gave answer:
"Yea, Cid! Without a doubt.
Give unto me your cavaliers all duly armed about.
Let them go in my keeping. Their safety I assure
As a lord to a good vassal; I make thee here secure

That they take no harm from any count or lesser baronet.
Here now in the assizes, a term for them I set,
That in the fields of Carrión at the end of three weeks' space
There duly in my presence the combat shall take place.
Who at the set time comes not, his suit is lost thereby,
From that time he is vanquished; for a traitor let him fly."
The two heirs of Carrión, by that decree they stand.
And thereupon my lord the Cid has kissed the King his hand;

"To thy hand are they delivered my cavaliers all three;
As to my King and Master I commend them unto thee.
They are ready now their duty to the full to undertake.
With honor to Valencia send them me for God his sake."
"So it be God's desire," answered the King and said.
The Cid the Campeador did off the helmet from his head,
Likewise the cap of linen as white as is the sun.
He freed his beard, the cord thereof he has forthwith undone.
Those in the court upon him, their full they could not gaze.
To the Counts Remónd and Henry forthwith he went his way.
And them closely he embraces and doth heartily require
To take of his possession all that suits with their desire.
These twain and many others who were persons of good will
He earnestly requested to take unto their fill
Some took his gifts, but others would not accept a thing.
The two hundred marks, he gave them once more unto the King.
Whatever was his pleasure he has taken of the rest:
"King, for love of the Creator one thing let me request.
Sire, with thy will I kiss thine hand. Since so these deeds are done,
And would fain unto Valencia which with great pain I won."

Then the Cid commanded to give sumpter-beasts unto the embassadors of the Heirs of Navarre and Aragon, and, moreover, to let them have whatever else they required.* And he sent them forth. The King don Alfonso with all the nobles of his court got on horseback in order to ride out with the Cid who was about to leave the town. When they came to Zocodover, the Cid being on his charger Baviéca, the King said to him:

"In faith, don Rodrigo, thou must now put spur to that charger of which I have heard most fair report."

The Cid smiled and said: "Sire, in thy court, are many, gentle and simple, who would gladly do such a thing. Bid them make sport with their steeds."

---

[5] Supplied like the former prose passage from the Chronicle of the Twenty Kings.

The King replied to him: "Cid, I am pleased with thine answer. Nevertheless I desire thee, for the love thou bearest me, to put that steed through his best paces."

CL.

The Cid then put spur to the charger and made him gallop
so fast that all were astonished at the career he ran.

The King with hand uplifted signed the cross upon his face.
"By San Isidro of León, I swear it by his grace
Is no nobleman so mighty our whole country o'er."
My lord Cid on the charger came then the King before,
And of his lord Alfonso there has he kissed the hand.
"To start fleet Baviéca thou gavest me command.
Today no Moor nor Christian has a horse so strong and swift.
Sire, unto thee I give him. Say thou wilt accept the gift."
Then said the King:
"No pleasure would I have therein indeed.
If I took him, then less glorious were the master of the steed.
But a horse like this befitteth too well a man like thee,
Swift to chase the Moors ye routed in the battle, when they flee.
Who that war-horse taketh from thee, God succor not again,
For by thee and by the charger to great honor we attain."
Their leave then have they taken. He left the Court forthright.

The Campeador most wisely counselled them who were to fight:
"Ha, Martin Antolínez! Per Vermudóz thou, too,
So likewise Muño Gustióz, my tried man and true.
Be resolute in combat like the gentlemen ye be.
See that of you good tidings in Valencia come to me."
Said Martin Antolínez: "Oh sire, what sayest thou?
For we must bear the burden we accepted even now.
Thou shalt hear naught of the vanquished, though haply of the slain."
He who in happy hour was born, thereof was glad and fain.
Of all his leave he taketh that for his friends are known.
Went my lord Cid to Valencia, and the King to Carrión.
But now the three weeks' respite of the term is past and o'er.
Lo! at the time appointed, they who serve the Campeador,
The debt their lord laid on them they were very fain to pay.
In safe-keeping of Alfonso, King of León, were they.
There for the Heirs of Carrión for two days' space they stayed.
With horses and caparisons, came the Heirs there well arrayed.

And in close compact with them have agreed their kinsmen all,
On the Campeador his henchmen, if in secret they might fall,
To slay them in the meadows, because their lords were silent.
They did not undertake it, though foul was their intent,
For of Alfonso of León they stood in mighty dread.

Watch o'er their arms they kept that night. And prayers to God they said.

At last has night passed over, and breaketh now the dawn,
And many worthy nobles there to the place have drawn,
For to behold that combat, wherefore their mirth was high.
Moreover King Alfonso above all men is by,
Since he desireth justice and that no wrong should be done.
The men of the good Campeador, they get their armour on.
All three are in agreement for one lord's men are they.
The Heirs of Carrión elsewhere have armed them for the fray.
The Count García Ordoñez sate with them in counsel there.
What suit they planned unto the King Alfonso they declare,
That neither should Coláda nor Tizón share in that war,
That in fight they might not wield them, who served the Campeador
That the brands were given over, they deemed a bitter ill;
Unto the King they told it. He would not do their will:

"When we held the court exception unto no sword did ye take;
But if ye have good weapons, your fortune they will make.
For them who serve the Campeador the swords e'en so will do.
Up, Carrión's Heirs, to battle now get you forth, ye two!
Like noblemen this combat, ye ought duly to achieve,
For the Campeador his henchmen naught undone therein will leave.
If forth, ye come victorious, then great shall be your fame;
But if that ye are vanquished, impute to us no blame.
All know ye sought it."
Carrión's Heirs were filled with grief each one.
And greatly they repented the thing that they had done.
Were it undone fain were they to give all Carrión's fee.

The henchmen of the Campeador are fully armed all three.
Now was the King Alfonso come forth to view them o'er.
Then spake to him the henchmen that served the Campeador:
"We kiss thy hands as vassals to their lord and master may,
'Twixt our party and their party thou shalt be judge this day.
For our succor unto justice but not to evil stand.
Here Carrión's Heirs of henchmen have gathered them a band.
What, or what not, we know not, that in secret they intend;
But our lord in thine hand left us our safety to defend.

For the love of the Creator justly maintain our part."
Said then the King in answer: "With all my soul and heart."
They brought for them the chargers of splendid strength and speed.
They signed the cross upon the selles. They leaped upon the steed.
The bucklers with fair bosses about their necks are cast.
And the keen pointed lances, in the hand they grip them fast.
Each lance for each man of the three doth its own pennon bear.
And many worthy nobles have gathered round them there.
To the field where were the boundaries, accordingly they went.
The three men of the Campeador were all of one intent,
That mightily his foeman to smite each one should ride.
Lo! were the Heirs of Carrión upon the other side,
With stores of men, for many of their kin were with the two.
The King has given them judges, justice and naught else to do,
That yea or nay they should not any disputation make.
To them where in the field they sate the King Alfonso spake:
"Hearken, ye Heirs of Carrión, what thing to you I say:
In Toledo ye contrived it, but ye did not wish this fray.
Of my lord Cid the Campeador I brought these knights all three
To Carrión's land, that under my safe-conduct they might be.
Wait justice. Unto evil no wise turn your intent.
Whoso desireth evil with force will I prevent;
Such a thing throughout my kingdom he shall bitterly bemoan."
How downcast were the spirits of the Heirs of Carrión!

Now with the King the judges have marked the boundaries out.
They have cleared all the meadow of people roundabout.
And unto the six champions the boundaries have they shown—
Whoever went beyond them should be held for overthrown.
The folk that round were gathered now all the space left clear;
To approach they were forbiddden within six lengths of a spear.
'Gainst the sun no man they stationed, but by lot gave each his place.
Forth between them came the judges, and the foes are face to face.
Of my lord Cid the henchmen toward the Heirs of Carrión bore,
And Carrión's Heirs against them who served the Campeador.
The glance of every champion fixes on his man forthright;
Before their breasts the bucklers with their hands have they gripped
    tight,
The lances with the pennons now have they pointed low,
And each bends down his countenance over the saddlebow;
Thereon the battle-chargers with the sharp spurs smote they,
And fain the earth had shaken where the steeds sprang away.
The glance of every champion fixes on his man forthright.
Three against three together now have they joined the fight.
Whoso stood round for certain deemed that they dead would fall.

Per Vermudóz the challenge who delivered first of all,
Against Ferránd Gonzálvez there face to face he sped.
They smote each other's bucklers withouten any dread.
There has Ferránd Gonzálvez pierced don Pero's target through.
Well his lance-shaft in two places he shattered it in two.
Unto the flesh it came not, for there glanced off the steel.
Per Vermudóz sat firmly, therefore he did not reel.
For every stroke was dealt him, the buffet back he gave,
He broke the boss of the buckler, the shield aside he drave.
He clove through guard and armour, naught availed the man his gear.
Nigh the heart into the bosom he thrust the battle-spear.
Three mail-folds had Ferrándo, and the third was of avail.
Two were burst through, yet firmly held the third fold of mail.
Ferrándo's shirt and tunic, with the unpierced iron mesh,
A handsbreadth by Per Vermudóz were thrust into the flesh.
And forth from his mouth straightway a stream of blood did spout.
His saddle-girths were broken; not one of them held out.
O'er the tail of the charger he hurled him to the ground.
That his death stroke he had gotten thought all the folk around.
He left the war-spear in him, set hand his sword unto.
When Ferránd Gonzálvez saw it, then well Tizón he knew.
He shouted, "I am vanquished," rather than the buffet bear.
Per Vermudóz, the judges so decreeing, left him there.

CLI.

With Dídago Gonzálvez now doth don Martin close
The spears. They broke the lances so furious were the blows.
Martin Antolínez on sword his hand he laid.
The whole field shone, so brilliant and flawless was the blade.
He smote a buffet. Sidewise it caught him fair and right.
Aside the upper helmet the glancing stroke did smite.
It clove the helmet laces. Through the mail-hood did it fall,
Unto the coif, hard slashing through coif and helm and all,
And scraped the hair upon his brow. Clear to the flesh it sped.
Of the helm a half fell earthward and half crowned yet his head.
When the glorious Coláda such a war-stroke had let drive,
Well knew Dídago Gonzálvez that he could not 'scape alive.
He turned the charger's bridle rein, and right about he wheeled.
A blade in hand he carried that he did not seek to wield.
From Martin Antolínez welcome with the sword he got.
With the flat Martin struck him. With the edge he smote him not.
Thereon that Heir of Carrión, a mighty yell he gave:
"Help me, Oh God most glorious, defend me from that glaive."
Wheeling his horse, in terror he fled before the blade.

The steed bore him past the boundary. On the field don Martin stayed.
Then said the King: "Now hither come unto my meinie.
Such a deed thou hast accomplished as has won this fight for thee."
That a true word he had spoken so every judge deemed well.

CLII.

The twain had won. Now let us of Muño Gustióz tell,
How with Ansuór Gonzálvez of himself account he gave.
Against each other's bucklers the mighty strokes they drave.
Was Ansuór Gonzálvez a gallant man of might.
Against don Muño Gustióz on the buckler did he smite,
And piercing through the buckler, right through the cuirass broke.
Empty went the lance; his body was unwounded by the stroke.
That blow struck, Muño Gustióz has let his buffet fly.
Through the boss in the middle was the buckle burst thereby.
Away he could not ward it. Through his cuirass did it dart.
Through one side was it driven though not nigh unto the heart.
Through the flesh of his body he thrust the pennoned spear,
On the far side he thrust it a full fathom clear.
He gave one wrench. Out of the selle that cavalier he threw.
Down to the earth he cast him, when forth the lance he drew.
And shaft and lance and pennon all crimson came they out.
All thought that he was wounded to the death without a doubt.
The lance he has recovered, he stood the foe above.
Said Gonzálvo Ansuórez: "Smite him not for God his love.
Now is won out the combat for all this game is done."
"We have heard defeat conceded," said the judges every one.
The good King don Alfonso bade them clear the field straightway.
For himself he took the armour upon it yet that lay.
In honor have departed they who serve the Campeador.
Glory be to the Creator, they have conquered in the war.
Throughout the lands of Carrión was sorrow at the height.
The King my lord Cid's henchmen has sent away by night,
That they should not be frightened or ambushed on the way,
Like men of prudent spirit they journeyed night and day.
Ho! in Valencia with the Cid the Campeador they stand.
On Carrión's Heirs of knavery the three have put the brand,
And paid the debt the lord Cid set upon them furthermore.
On that account right merry was the Cid Campeador.
Upon the heirs of Carrión is come a mighty smirch.
Who flouts a noble lady and leaves her in the lurch,
May such a thing befall him, or worse fortune let him find.
Of Carrión's Heirs the dealings let us leave them now behind.
For what has been vouchsafed them now were they all forlorn.

Of this man let us make mention who in happy hour was born.
And great are the rejoicings through Valencia the town,
Because the Campeador his men had won such great renown.
His beard their lord Roy Diaz hard in his hand has ta'en:
"Thanks to the King of Heaven, well are 'venged my daughters twain.
Now may they hold their Carrión lands. Their shame is wiped away.
I will wed them in great honor, let it grieve whom it may."

They of Navarre and Aragon were busied now to treat,
And with Alfonso of León in conference they meet.
Dame Sol and Dame Elvíra in due course wedded are.
Great were their former matches, but these are nobler far.
He gave with greater honor than before the twain to wed;
He who in happy hour was born still doth his glory spread,
Since o'er Navarre and Aragon as queens his daughters reign;
Today are they kinswomen unto the kings of Spain.
From him came all that honor who in good hour had birth.
The Cid who ruled Valencia has departed from the earth
At Pentecost. His mercy may Christ to him extend.
To us all, just men or sinners, may He yet stand our friend.
Lo! the deeds of the Cid Campeador! Here takes the book an end.

Echo Library

www.echo-library.com

Echo Library uses advanced digital print-on-demand technology to build and preserve an exciting world class collection of rare and out-of-print books, making them readily available for everyone to enjoy.

Situated just yards from Teddington Lock on the River Thames, Echo Library was founded in 2005 by Tom Cherrington, a specialist dealer in rare and antiquarian books with a passion for literature.

Please visit our website for a complete catalogue of our books, which includes foreign language titles.

The Right to Read

Echo Library actively supports the Royal National Institute of the Blind's Right to Read initiative by publishing a comprehensive range of large print and clear print titles.

Large Print titles are in 16 point Tiresias font as recommended by the RNIB.

Clear Print titles are in 13 point Tiresias font and designed for those who find standard print difficult to read.

Customer Service

If there is a serious error in the text or layout please send details to feedback@echo-library.com and we will supply a corrected copy. If there is a printing fault or the book is damaged please refer to your supplier.